Becoming the
ULTIMATE
Human

Kenny Garcia

Becoming the Ultimate Human

KENNY GARCIA

For my Family

Reviews

THIS BOOK IS DESIGNED TO SPARK THE
DIVINE INTELLIGENCE INSIDE EVERYONE!
AMAZING WORK KENNY GARCIA!

Billy Carson / 4biddenknowledge – 2x Best Selling Author

AMAZING CONTENT. KENNY GARCIA IS A
TRUE INSPIRATION. I LOOK FORWARD TO
DIGGING DEEPER INTO MEDITATIONS
BECAUSE OF THIS BOOK.

Elisabeth Hoekstra Best Selling Author – The Recipe to
Elevated Consciousness.

"NEXT LEVEL SPIRITUAL MEDICINE!! LOTS OF
INFO IN THIS BOOK!!!"

Donny Arcade – Billboard Artist

Contents

Foreword   xi

Introduction   xiii

1. AWAKENINGS   1
   My Awakening   6

2. FIRST, LOVE YOURSELF   19
   FLY

3. SHADOW WORK   25

4. DENSITIES   33

5. PARAMAHANSA YOGANANDA   39

6. MAHASAMADHI   49
   The Eight Limbs of Yoga   50
   Mahasamadhi   57

7. MEDITATION   63
   Cosmic Energy   65
   What You Can Expect   67
   Science-Based Benefits   71
   The Perfect Posture   72
   The Fogging a Mirror Method   73

8. THE MAHARISHI EFFECT   79

9. HUMANITY   83

10. THE BREATH   99

11. THE ULTIMATE PATH   113

Acknowledgments   129

About the Author   131

Social Media   133

Foreword

Throughout history, the quest for enlightenment has been a deeply rooted notion and sought-after goal.

The world we live in, our current understanding of the universe, and what it means to be human, are constantly evolving. Along the course of this evolution, knowledge helps us reach higher and higher levels of understanding and connectivity.

This book is your guide to embarking on a journey towards personal growth and understanding—one where you will explore the depths of your being, examine the obstacles that may be impeding your journey, and discover what true enlightenment looks like within a 21st-century lens.

Through theory and practical application, this book will equip you with the tools you'll need to begin your path toward becoming an empowered individual and fully realizing your highest potential.

Kenny Garcia masterfully breaks down the ancient wisdom in ways that anyone can understand.

May we all discover true enlightenment in our own ways!

Billy Carson
    4biddenknowledge Inc
    Best Selling Author
    Compendium Of The Emerald Tablets
    Woke Doesn't Mean Broke

Introduction

For as long as I can remember, I have been fascinated by the mysteries of this world. What exactly are we? Where did we come from? Why is it that we still do not know or understand many things? The world of spirit and paranormal activities has always intrigued me and piqued my interest as a child. I had heard other members of my family talk about the spirit world, ghosts, and spirituality, but those concepts were too far-fetched for a seven-year-old to grasp. Nevertheless, that is most likely when my spiritual journey began.

As a young child, I remember being captivated by UFOs, extraterrestrials, spirits, apparitions, heaven and hell, God, the devil, and everything in between.

However, growing up in a Colombian, Catholic household, I believed many of the things my family taught me. My grandmother, who has always been deeply religious, instilled these beliefs in me and my cousins at a young age. We were taught how important prayer is, that God and the devil exist, that there is good and evil in the world, and that bad behavior can send you to hell.

My cousins and I believed all of these things because we were thinking with the mind of a child.

Unfortunately, accepting these beliefs will cause a person to live a life of fear. I was afraid of the spirit world and the unknown as a child, and I thought that God would punish me for every tiny mistake or wrongdoing.

In the end, my life experiences helped me get over these limiting beliefs and gave me answers to the mystifying questions I had as a child.

These conflicts stayed with me through my experiences in elementary school, junior high, and high school. As I grew older and more mature, I came to realize that adults do not have all the answers and they don't know as much as we as kids thought they did.

No one does.

Everyone is just doing their best, trying to get by, survive, or advance in life.

In my teenage years, I felt that nobody had figured it out, not even my parents. I remember thinking to myself, "They're older than me; they're raising me; they always know what to do, surely they have the answers to life." I soon realized that was not the case.

As I grew older, I began to question my reality, wondering why certain things were the way they were. I realized that neither my mother nor my father had the answers I was looking for. Most people had no idea! Not my older brother, older cousins, or any of my aunts and uncles. No one had a true understanding of these things.

It appeared as if everyone just went through life on autopilot believing in the famous saying, "you never know".

I'm sure we have all gone through this in our own ways. Now, here is the good news: as magnificent beings of light, we are all destined to awaken at some point.

Our awakening represents an experience that shakes the foundation of who we are, shatters our reality, turns our lives upside down, and forces us to ask ourselves some soul-searching questions, such as, "Who the hell am I? What role does God play in this? Why am I even here? Why do I suffer and go through pain? Why is there so much evil in the world? Where is this all heading towards?"

The world is filled with so much craziness that it often feels as if we are living in an inverted universe. At least, that's what it seems like as we continue living through each day in this bizarre world we call normal.

What does normal even mean?

Normalcy does not exist. People are just people, and all people operate differently. Does it make sense that if a large number of people agree that something is true, then everyone else is required to accept it as true?

When a certain number of people believe something to be true, it affects the mass consciousness of humanity, making it possible for other people to believe in it as well. This type of phenomenon is referred to as the "100th monkey effect." When an individual conceives an idea or a new way of doing something that has never been done before, this new idea goes up into the collective consciousness grid of humanity. This makes it possible for anyone else within humanity to tap into this newly conceived idea or experience because all our minds are connected to each other via this consciousness grid that encompasses the entire planet Earth. So, a few decades and generations of believing in the same old belief system makes humanity accept the fallacy that certain things have always been this way. Old belief systems have become immutable facts in the minds of many. But the truth is that there is always a lot more to life than we have been made to believe and apparently, no one has the answers to life's mysterious questions. Or do they!?

Is it possible that there are actual beings on this planet that have discovered the answers to these questions? When it comes to the big questions of life, do we ever really find the answers, or do we just keep asking them from one generation to the next?

Fundamentally, we may be asking the right questions, but as a collective, we have not been open enough to finding the right answers. Is it possible that there are intelligent beings on this planet who can understand these puzzles and share their knowledge so that we can solve them?

Sometimes, it does seem like the only people who can dependably offer meaning to these questions are lonely hermits who live high up in the mountains. Are these people the only humans who can reach higher levels of awareness?

Even these secluded individuals know that once they reach a higher level of awareness, they cannot just step off their mountaintops in front of billions of people and say, "Hey guys, I've found the answers to life! This is what it is. Believe in me!" They know such grandstanding will not work. Even though they have acquired many truths, they are mindful that trying to put themselves on that kind of platform will never work because different levels of awareness separate humanity's ability to communicate and comprehend cosmic knowledge.

We are all equal at the level of our souls, but, unfortunately in our current collective human state, we are all separate vibrationally, mentally, emotionally, and intellectually. We all have different levels of intelligence, or, if you prefer, awareness. The level of awareness you have reached so far in this life determines what you can understand, how well you can understand it, and how well you can express your intelligence.

You will not understand higher knowledge until you raise your frequency of intelligence. How exactly do we go about doing this!? Fortunately, we do not have to live like hermits on mountaintops to find our level of awareness and develop it to its fullest.

So then, how do we increase our intelligence, our awareness? To answer that question, we must first understand the mechanics of physical reality and how it is constructed.

It is no secret that we live in a reality made entirely of light and energy. Scientists have already demonstrated this. Energy cannot be created or destroyed. It is limitless, it is eternal, and it can only change its form.

Before you can understand how to maximize your intelligence, you need to know that everything is made up of energy, vibration, and frequency. For the time being, we will concentrate on these three things because all matter is energy vibrating at a certain frequency. These three components are what create physical and spiritual matter. The denser the matter, the lower the frequency and the more solid matter becomes. The higher the frequency is, the more flexible matter becomes, the less solid it appears, and the more easily you can change it.

If you raise the vibrational frequency of your mind, you

will be able to tap in and access/download higher levels of understanding, and higher thought patterns.

To begin this journey, you must first recognize that your mind is not your brain, as many of us were taught as children. Our brains are actually more like physical receivers for the thoughts being conceived from the higher mind.

Our mind is a field of energy that encompasses the entire human body and it is aware of itself, making it conscious. Your mind is a field of energy that vibrates at a certain frequency. Your thoughts can literally be measured in frequency in real time. Because of this, your mind can only comprehend, and communicate so much information depending upon the frequency at which it vibrates.

When people have negative thought patterns such as fear, insecurity, shame, pessimism, animosity, and so on, their minds vibrate at a lower frequency. Higher-frequency thoughts are more common in people who are naturally loving, kind, compassionate, empathetic, and supportive. As a result, higher-frequency thoughts are more cohesive, centered, harmonious, and connected, and they tend to include everyone's needs.

So, then the question becomes, "How do I *raise* the frequency of my intelligence?" Further, we are led to ask, "What do I have to do for my mind to vibrate at this higher frequency, in order for me to access and download higher knowledge?" Such are the questions we will cover in this book.

Guys, I believe that if we want to reach our full potential as human beings, we need to figure out what the pinnacle of human existence is and how to get there so that we can express ourselves in the purest, most crystalline form possible—like the true gods and goddesses we all are but have been programmed to believe otherwise.

How does a person with a fully functioning brain become the best human they can be? What does that process look like? How does a person get there?

Most of the answers to these questions are found in the world of *Spirit* and meditation is what brings you to that world—a world of interconnectedness, beauty, equality, power, and mindfulness.

To enter this world, you must learn how to achieve stillness of the mind, also known as the meditative state of being. When people reach this level they become avatars by their own right through consistency and discipline.

The closer we get to our spiritual selves, the more the natural world will conform to our conscious intentions. We learn how to become one with nature's forces while respecting the natural world and achieving a level of awareness that is in harmony with nature.

You can access the depths of your subconscious mind if you maintain focus and observation on the natural inhalation/exhalation process of the breath via your diaphragm. All the answers to the problems you face in life are in the depths of your inner self. If you turn your attention inward, you can get to those depths and start building the skills you need to become the ultimate human.

The entire history of humanity is encoded in your DNA. Your genes represent the strands and tides of not only all of humanity but also a more specific, familial bloodline that is locked inside of you. Everything your ancestors have ever done—whether they have raved, killed, given life, created, or conceived amazing ideas that changed the world—everything they have ever experienced—the best and the worst, the happiest and the saddest — is written into your DNA.

The *deoxyribonucleic acid* in your genes is a repository for this mixture of ancient bloodlines and peoples who lived before you. You are them, but you are also something completely unique and original.

When you quiet your mind through meditation and reach a deeper level of consciousness, your soul begins to reveal its original and distinctive character. When you do this, you begin to unravel the DNA within you. All the answers you have ever been looking for are drawn like magnets to your questions, energetically popping up in front of you.

Answers and solutions will come steadily if you are steadfastly meditating, but you must be patient. You must keep at it, strive with great diligence, and meditate every day for this to happen.

You need to be able to turn your attention inward, concentrate on your breathing, and shut out all other ideas and distractions. Keep your gaze focused inward, listening for the whispers of your consciousness.

For this to be successful, you must have complete control over your breath.

It has been my hope to present this book as a quick, light guide for your spiritual journey. For the last sixteen years, I have worked diligently to integrate cosmic awareness into my life, discovering a lot of forward-thinking ideas along the way. I am a person who has successfully traversed the astral plane many times throughout my meditation journey, consciously. As a result, these experiences have given me a more expanded outlook on the nature of reality and our connection to this experience we call life.

The astral plane transports those who are in the deepest states of consciousness across the celestial boundaries. Moving beyond the confines of time and space, their *Spirit* achieves levels of consciousness and interconnectedness with other beings only attained by those who practice the highest levels of meditation.

Also, I am a person who has had personal experiences with both physical and non-physical beings and other inexplicable phenomena. In the sixteen years since I learned about meditation, I have experienced countless miracles and wonders that were previously beyond my understanding.

Who I am at my core has been profoundly altered by the passage of time. I am no longer the carefree young man I used to be. At this point in my life, I am unrecognizable from my past.

The way I think and learn is radically different. I even speak and interact with others differently than before. I do not view human beings the same. I see the energy and vibes of an individual over their physical attributes. Transformatively, I am not the person I used to be; rather, I have become someone completely new, distinct, and recast as a more self-realized being of light.

We are all different than we were ten years ago. That is a simple, universal truth.

However, many of us continue to be trapped in the same lifestyle patterns. Easily, some of us become stuck in self-constructed loops that take us nowhere. I, myself, was looping for a whole decade without even realizing it and it took a lot to break free and realize this. What is disheartening is that sometimes there are loops within loops, and people keep looping unproductively throughout their entire lives, doing the same thing over and over again while para-doxically expecting a different outcome.

After all, that is the definition of insanity, right?

You cannot keep doing things at the same frequency of perception and expect a higher frequency result; that does not work. That is not how energy, vibration, and frequency work.

The link between these three things is due to the abso-lute fact that like *attracts* like. You can only perceive and experience your own frequency. You cannot perceive anything that vibrates higher than you. If by chance you do encounter something vibrating at a higher frequency than you, you will not understand the encounter. For you to understand that experience, your mind must be operating at a higher frequency of understanding.

My goal in writing these things is to help and guide you in finding the answers to the questions, "How do I become the best version of myself that I can be in this life?" And, "How am I going to get there?"

Everyone is on their own journey. No one's purpose is more important than others. Everyone's life purpose is equally important, and we each hold within our souls a unique puzzle piece to the complete image of God.

By the way, there is no such thing as being "too late."

We all move forward on our own accord. Never judge others for failing to understand what you know or want to know. The cosmic clock ticks differently for each one of us. Everyone lives their life at a different pace and on a different level. We should honor that difference, respect it, see it for what it is, and not judge it in our minds. Each one of us can set the goal to keep moving forward with love and intelligence.

Now, let me bring everything I have been talking about full circle. If you continue to read and want to know everything in this book, then you, my friend, my beautiful brother and sister of light, are ready to understand who you are and what your human potential is. You are ready to put an end to your suffering, to understand, and to gain more wisdom, experience, knowledge, and intelligence. You are also prepared for everything that comes with it because we all know that life is not always full of flowers and beauty.

When there are ups, there will be some downs. That is the very nature of duality. But I hope that by fully integrating all the information in this book, you will learn how to save yourself from the dualistic nature of the world by gaining a holistic understanding of Yin and Yang, and other polarities. This will help you bring your left and right brain hemispheres into harmony, so you see the world as it really is—neutral.

Everything, absolutely everything, vibrates at a neutral frequency, regardless of how good or bad you believe it is from your human mind's perspective. Your personal life experiences and the people who most influenced your life are what shaped your belief system, which determines whether something is good or bad, positive or negative. However, in its true, authentic form, it is a neutral backdrop.

Nothing without a foundation has any significance. Life is fundamentally meaningless. However, that does not mean life is *absolutely* meaningless. On the contrary, life has meaning because of you, the human being. You give meaning to every experience. You decide whether it is good or bad. It makes no difference whether others agree with you or not; it is what it is. Everything we see and experience is neutral, but our belief systems determine whether it is good or bad.

I understand that there are some experiences in our lives that are so heartbreaking, evil, and negative that you may wonder, "How could that be a neutral experience? It was true. It was extremely painful for me. It had a significant impact on my life." To question in this manner is entirely understandable.

However, you must recognize that there are certain things over which you have no control and that they are simply part of the substantives of life that you must navigate. Some experiences are the result of contracts made between our souls and the universe before we were born. One example would be your parents' divorce when you were very young. Perhaps you, like me, have no recollection of your mother and father ever sleeping in the same bed together. My parents divorced when I was two years old. You, like me, have no control over something like that, so you say, "Okay, well, my parents divorced when I was two, and I suffered a lot of problems, as a result, growing up. How can this be a positive experience? How can this be a neutral experience?"

You must understand that certain experiences in this life are beyond your control, particularly as a child. These are things that your soul understood it had to go through before becoming incarnate in this life. Many things that occur to you in life, the soul chooses for its own development, and much of what you go through is also karmically tied to the actions of your previous life. Accepting how the soul comes to be part of humanity is a very important idea. Your acceptance allows you to know what you will face in life.

What I've come to realize from my own personal spiritual experiences, is that before you even come to Earth, your soul chooses your parents, your birthplace and environment, your upbringing, as well as the paths you take and the people you meet, so that you can do the job that your soul has for you on this planet. In addition, you will have to live up to the terms of certain contracts, especially if they involve karmic debts from a previous life that must be paid for in this life. For these types of experiences, it would feel as if you have no control over it. Like the example of your growing up with divorced parents since you were two years old, you could not have prevented that from happening at such a young age; it was simply part of your soul's path in this lifetime.

But when you reach the point where you are a conscious creator and consciously bring about the experiences you imagine in your mind, you will start to see things in a new way. You will see that, in the end, everything is neutral. At that point, you will find significance in everything and everyone, including your parents' divorce when you were two years old.

Looking back at the person you are today, you may see your life with divorced parents as a positive thing. Because, as you see, if they had not divorced, you would not have become the person you are today.

I hope you understand that you can always look back on something you initially viewed as a negative experience or memory and find the good, the purpose, and the meaning behind why it happened. Then you can feel a little relieved that it happened because it shaped you into the person you are today.

Now that you guys have seen a little bit of how I think, how I express myself, and which things I am passionate about, I think it is best to get into the real subject of this book, which is how to become the ultimate human.

What does this look like? And where do we start? Let's figure it out together!

Musical Vibes for this chapter
Search: **CrewZ - Transition**
https://song.link/i/1465340399

Awakenings

I BELIEVE that the universe will place my book in the hands of those who are ready to read it. If you are reading this book, it means you have either already gone through your awakening process, are in the thick of it now, or are about to go through it.

With great excitement, I believe this book may be the catalyst and facilitator for your awakening. You would not be on the path to finding and becoming the best version of yourself if you had not had some kind of spiritual awakening before buying this book. So, hello, and welcome to the rest of your life.

I AM NOT sure what happened in your life to cause your awakening. I do not know your age, what gender you identify with, where you are in the world as you read this, or what time it is.

What I do know is that you are a part of me.

What I do know is that we are connected, and our

connection transcends space and time. We are infinite, and whatever year you were finally able to read this book, that is the year, time, and date down to the second that you were meant to read it.

This book was brought to you as a result of your awakening. It brought you to this very moment, where you are reading these words that my mind is sharing with you. For that, I am eternally grateful.

I thank *Spirit* for directing you to this chapter of my book. I am grateful for your life, for your awakening, because it shows that humanity is becoming more conscious of who they are and their connection to *Spirit*, God, the universe, the creator, all that is.

It is beyond description.

It is a formidable sensation.

It is an inexplicable presence.

Above all, it is intelligence and unconditional love. I have come to realize through my life experiences, that unconditional love is the highest frequency of intelligence you can align yourself to. If you do not already know why, you will soon find out. Love produces the most harmonious manifestations.

Once again, I am deeply grateful for your awakening because it will transform you into the ultimate human. That is, if it is a path you choose for yourself in this lifetime. You are not obligated to make this your life. Everyone is different, and everyone deserves to be distinct and unique.

For the sake of this book that is now in your hands, or perhaps you are listening to it as an audiobook, or perhaps you are just reading the text on some screen somewhere, I cannot thank you enough for your eyes or ears gracing these words. I adore and value each and every one of you. I believe that now, more than ever, we deserve to be happy and healthy, as well as to know and understand the truth about who we are, where we came from, and where we are going.

Let us turn back to examine your awakening.

It was not exactly beautiful, was it? Most likely, you were forced to examine your life and come to terms with the fact that you had been living a lie for the majority of your existence. You were led to believe something that was not entirely accurate about yourself or life in general. You now understand that there is far more to life than you were led to believe. There is far more to you than you have been led to believe. There is more to who you are, what you can under-stand, and what you can create than you were taught.

As a result of this new understanding, you find yourself wanting answers. You want to know and understand more. You want to have more experience. You want to know the truth because you are tired of the lies, the manipulation, and simply not being happy and fulfilled.

It does not really matter whether you have all the money in the world, have traveled the world five times, or have invested in everything possible. You can boast about all these things, yet there is still something missing inside of you. There is still a gap somewhere in all of your greatness or wealth.

Or maybe you are not so materially blessed and come from humble beginnings, and you are still stuck in this rat race, unsure of where to go from here. It does not make a difference where any one of us is in terms of our journey, because ultimately, we are all at different points along the path.

What matters is that you have experienced or are experiencing your awakening. What happens next is going to be breathtaking. However, as you approach that beautiful reality, it can and will become ugly. You must be willing to accept that during this awakening process.

You will be forced to confront your demons and all of the emotions you have kept bottled up inside since childhood. You must be willing to confront and bring to the surface of your conscious mind what you have chosen to bury deep within your subconscious. That includes those things that you chose to forget because they were too painful or because you simply did not understand them.

Now that you are awakening, you have no choice but to revisit these old patterns, memories, and experiences that have hurt you for so long. It is only when you choose to bring these experiences back to the conscious mind that you can begin to extract their meaning.

You start extracting intelligence from within. Because of that, you gain more wisdom and understanding, which makes it easier for you to embrace your awakening.

Remember that you are a spiritual being first, having a physical experience second. Your primary reality is your internal reality. Your secondary reality is your external reality, which is a reflection of what is going on within you.

Because you are a spiritual being first and foremost, it makes no difference what material experiences or possessions you have. You will still have a hole in your life, feeling unfulfilled and as if something is missing. You have reached a stalemate and are bored, despite having all the money in the world.

Why is this the case? I believe it is because you are too engrossed in your secondary reality, your external reality. You do not have time, and you have made no time, to be still and reconnect with your primary reality, which is your internal reality.

As a result, something remains missing in your life.

Remember that you are a spiritual being first and a human being second. You have been so focused on your human life and pleasures that you have completely ignored the spiritual part of you, which is your true form. As a result, yes, something is still lacking in your life. That connection to the divine.

It makes no difference whether you are wealthy, impoverished, or somewhere in between. If you keep your attention on the outside world, on your human life, you will always reach a plateau. You will always feel as if something is missing. You will always feel like your money is not enough. Money is insufficient. The love of another human being is insufficient. Having a family is insufficient. Traveling and gaining experience is insufficient.

Finally, you must fulfill the spiritual aspect of your being because it is your true essence. At your core, you are *Spirit*.

Upon realizing this, you must decide to incorporate *Spirit* more comprehensively into your life.

Consider doing more things in alignment with your Spirit that can help uplift you. Things like meditation, chanting, going for walks in nature, and reading self-help and empowerment books like this one. If you already have money and are just now waking up, you have a slight advantage because you can use it to travel to ancient sites around the world. You have the advantage of being able to travel to places that make you feel good and help you learn, grow, and understand their spiritual aspects. If you do not have the financial means to travel, you can still do your research in all of these different places on the internet. You do not need to go there to understand it. You can learn about and conduct research on almost anything by virtually traveling anywhere in the world. You simply must be willing to put in the effort.

I WOULD LIKE to share my own personal awakening story with you. What caused me to reach this level of intelligence? What prompted me to want to learn more about becoming the ultimate human? What drove me to devote the last sixteen years of my life to meditation? Why am I doing this for all of you? Why did I write this book in the first place?

Let me begin at the beginning so you can get a better understanding of where I am coming from. You might be able to relate to my story, or you might not. It is my hope that my story will inspire and motivate you to keep going, because we all have a past that we either regret or wish we could change.

As you know, you cannot change the past. You can only move forward from where you are now. Every moment is a new moment. From the moment you wake up today, you are no longer the person you were yesterday. Every day and every moment is a brand new you. It is my desire that by learning about my awakening, you will understand what I mean.

MY AWAKENING

My spiritual awakening began in earnest when I graduated from high school in May of 2007. But before this big turning point in my life, I had a smaller but still important awakening a couple of years earlier. As a young teen, my mind became occupied with ideas about paranormal ETs, UFOs, the government, and cover-ups. By the time I was sixteen, I decided that everything I thought I knew about life was a lie, which emboldened me to start digging deeply into classified, top-secret government documents.

I reviewed what seemed like thousands of hours' worth of testimony from whistleblowers that had been made public by Project Camelot. Project Camelot was an online platform that was hosted in 2006 by both Kerry Cassidy and Bill Ryan. On this platform, the two of them conducted interviews with hundreds of whistleblowers who had worked on top secret government projects and risked their lives to tell the truth about their experiences.

I was also digging into many interviews within the Conscious Media Network, hosted by Regina Meredith.

This was amazing information a teenager should not have been getting into, especially in the early 2000s when no other teens were, or so I thought. Because I was so fascinated by it, I just knew that I was the only one digging into these things, and that idea seemed to excite me unbelievably.

In May of 2007, when I was eighteen years old, I was introduced to the spiritual realm and meditation. Meditation and spirituality really sped up the frequency of my consciousness and intelligence, making me wiser and able to understand more than I could have ever imagined.

Let me start this story by explaining my lifestyle at this time. At the age of eighteen, my lifestyle consisted of smoking a lot of weed, going out and having fun, drinking, and making stupid decisions. As a senior in high school, I did not care about spirituality, gaining intelligence, or learning about the mysteries of life and why we are all here. I did not have the willingness to comprehend life-altering concepts.

The only things that interested me were girls, looking as cool as possible, and having as much fun as possible. That was all I could think about. Then all of this wild living stopped when my bad eating habits and uncontrolled partying caused my small intestines to get tangled up. I had been eating junk food late at night and not giving my digestive system enough time to process it before going to sleep, which led to digestive issues.

Ironically, I was also a big fan of working out at the time. Despite my unhealthy lifestyle, I looked great physically. Growing up, I was always an athlete. I played soccer for eight years, and I had always been athletic and interested in physical activities.

As a result, my body did not appear as if I led an unhealthy lifestyle. However, the fact remained that I was living stupidly and not making the best choices for my physical and spiritual health. What happened to me in the summer of 2007 after graduation was extremely damaging. Even though I went through something terrible, it woke me up and helped me grow into the man I am today.

It all began the day one of my younger cousins came up to me and said, "Hey, I have two girls who want to go to the movies tonight on a date." I had no idea who these girls were, so it was like going on a blind date. When you are young and single, all you care about is having fun, so you might think, "Hey, that's cool. Let's go have some fun and get to know these girls." That is when my world began to shift.

At the time, I was living with my father in South Florida, but my mother was visiting from up north. While driving in her car with her, I suddenly felt this strange pulling sensation on the left side of my belly button, which caused a shortness of breath to the point where I felt like I was not getting any oxygen. In that instance, I remembered that the night before, while being extremely high off weed and doing my thing in the wee hours of the morning, I had experienced the exact same thing. I had a strange tugging sensation close to the right side of my belly button that caused extreme pain in my stomach. I was so committed to working out at the time, my first instinct was to start doing pushups. Almost immediately after doing pushups, the pain stopped. I forgot about it, went to sleep, and it was as if it had never happened.

But this time I was in my mother's car, getting ready for my double-blind date, and the pain was becoming stronger, causing shortness of breath. I turned to my mother and said, "Mom, I'm not sure what's wrong with my stomach, but I can't breathe. I can't take this pain. Please take me to the hospital."

This occurred on a Friday. I was admitted to the hospital for four days, during which time I was not allowed to eat anything. The only fluids I was allowed came through an IV, and for four, unbearably long days I was pumped with IV bag after IV bag while constantly having to empty my bladder. I went to the hospital weighing a solid one-hundred-fifty pounds of mostly muscle, but I came out four days later weighing a terrifying one-hundred-twenty-eight pounds. Unbelievably, I had lost twenty-two pounds in four days!

The doctors finally figured out that I had experienced a volvulus entanglement of my small intestines. This is a condition in which the intestinal tubes twist and get stuck, often leading to infections in the digestive system. According to my doctor, it is something more common in children and very unusual to see in someone my age at the time.

The doctor inquired as to whether I knew what had caused it. Of course, I lied and said I had no idea. But the truth was that I had been eating and sleeping poorly all week, every single day leading up to that Friday.

I was going to bed munching on junk food all night, falling to sleep at three or four in the morning, and not allowing my body to properly digest food.

The infection moved into my digestive system, jamming up my small intestine and ultimately causing massive weight loss.

Imagine this: I was a high school senior who had just graduated and should have been full of energy and enthusiasm for the summer ahead.

Instead, I was depressed because I had lost twenty-two pounds and had no muscle mass.

Here I stood, underweight, very tired, and weak, feeling miserable all the time. I had no idea what to do with my life and was constantly asking why God was punishing me.

Soul-searching questions plagued my mind as I began to ask, "What exactly did I do to deserve this? I just graduated from high school; don't I deserve to have fun with my life? Why am I having this experience right now? Why did I lose so much weight? Why am I feeling so fragile? Why do I feel like I'm about to die?"

Those were exhausting questions for someone so young to ask.

I was now living in my new reality.

I found it hard to eat, to even get hungry, or to understand what had just happened. My body looked different and felt different. It was a nightmare come true.

The beauty of this experience is that my desperate need for physical healing brought me to the practice of meditation.

I recall sitting in my room one day-on the phone with my mother as she argued with me, urging me to take the prescription drugs that the hospital had given me, but I have been opposed to pharmaceutical drugs ever since I was young.

I did not believe in them.

I did not trust the side effects of pharmaceutical drugs.

The fact that drug companies would stress their side effects made me distrust them, as if they were complete nonsense and there was something more nefarious about them.

I felt there was some hidden agenda that I simply did not understand at the time. The result was that I did not take any of the medicines the hospital gave me for my intestines.

Despite this attitude toward medicine, I did believe in natural holistic healing even before I was eighteen years old. Perhaps I did not understand everything, but regarding the power of healing, I was convinced there were many things incomprehensible to most people.

For the time being, I just did not understand what it was all about. While the science seemed elusive, I was aware of its presence. Something instinctively told me that there was more to healing than just taking these stupid prescription drugs.

I went to work wanting to learn everything I could, so I looked online right away for natural ways to heal the body. What would be a natural, holistic way for me to heal?

During my research, I came across a lengthy article on meditation. It was the random nature of my thoughts that prompted me to read this article in the first place.

Late at night, I began thinking to myself, "What exactly is meditation?"

"What motivates Hindus, Buddhists, and other Asian spiritualists to do this?"

"Is it really just sitting there going "ohm" and feeling more peaceful and quiet in your mind that suddenly enables you to heal your high blood pressure and anxiety?"

"There must be more to it than I understand."

Questions flooded my mind.

I was determined to read this lengthy article all the way through. I am happy I did because I learned that anyone can heal themselves of almost anything by regularly following the simple steps of meditation.

Desperate to get better, I started to put my faith in every remedy that promised instant, amazing, or profound changes. As a result, I began to believe, without question, what I was reading.

Even though I believed it, my mind and ego were skeptical.

I asked, "How can someone heal themselves through meditation?"

To my mind, that simply did not make sense. Yet, I was eager to learn it and did not care as long as it promised to bring healing. I was willing to give it a shot and was not bothered by what other people thought of me.

Desperation drove me forward.

Jump ahead a couple of weeks with me. At the time, YouTube was just getting up to speed, but it was already becoming popular. I started watching YouTube videos on meditation, learning more about it.

One day, I came across a one-hour animated video called Spiritual Reality narrated by Ashish Vidyarthi. This video changed my life forever. It covered a lot of information, which added to my desire to learn everything I could.

He talked about meditation, cosmic energy, healing, astral projection, enlightenment, and other things. I watched the entire video at once. It was so beautiful to watch that I could not take my eyes off it and became obsessed with learning how to meditate. Over the years I must have directed over 1,000 humans to this particular video.

This video gave me all the proof I needed to convince my logical mind that using these ancient meditation techniques was the way to get healthy again. I was also exposed to other techniques for healthy living, such as controlling diaphragmatic breathing and manipulating the power of cosmic energy.

Inspired by my discovery, I began meditating right away and the first thing that struck me was how impatient I was. Each day when I started to meditate, it took me about thirty minutes just to calm down. I had watched the video, but I still did not fully understand how diaphragmatic breathing or other similar techniques worked.

Please realize that I had no foundation for understanding these things. Social media then was nothing like it is today. There was no conscious community and I had no mentors to ask for guidance. I literally had to become my own mentor. The only thing I was aware of was the desire to restore health to my body, and I was prepared to take any action necessary to achieve this goal.

To accomplish this, I made it a habit to breathe deeply

three times a day for thirty minutes at a time. After a while, I observed that it took me significantly less time than thirty minutes to calm my thoughts.

I went from thirty minutes to twenty minutes to five minutes. Eventually, I got to the point where I could quiet my mind in under a minute. As a result, I learned how to breathe through my diaphragm in order to live a healthier life.

Every time I listened to my diaphragm inhale and exhale, I noticed a difference in the sounds it made. The larger intake of oxygen caused me to listen carefully to its sounds, and in doing so, my mind became relaxed. By being consistent every day, I taught myself how to enter a meditative state of being.

Soon, I found myself meditating for an hour to an hour and a half in a completely thoughtless state of being. I wouldn't move a muscle and would get completely lost into the expansiveness I would feel in my head. It was such a euphoric feeling! I also began having profound experiences dealing with Spirit realm. I was doing this practically every day, at least four or five days a week, for over two months consistently.

I began to notice that my stomach would not get as bloated as it previously had after a meal. Within weeks, I could eat almost whatever I wanted as well as work out again, feeling stronger and stronger. (In later years, my workouts became less and less a part of my routine, but nowadays, I am back at it!)

Thanks to my regular meditations and the great cosmic energies I was getting, my digestive system started to get stronger. These pervasive changes enabled me to realize that meditation is a science and that miracles can happen in the body. It was true as long as I stayed consistent and constant in my new found beliefs. In any case, it was true for me because these were the new experiences that were dramatically and comprehensively changing my life.

Everything that happened after that experience in 2007 has shaped me into the man I am today. It has been sixteen years since that happened. It is easy to be thankful in retrospect for the hospital experience. I am grateful for discovering meditation in the manner in which I did, because it humbled me. It made me realize that life is short and that you never know when you will die. At least, that is what I thought at the time. It made me fall in love with life again, as well as with a beautiful, spiritual practice that I realized would be a part of me for the rest of my life.

Because meditation changed my life for the better, I felt compelled to tell everyone else about its benefits. It was an incredible feeling, and I appreciated it for what it was. I knew everyone else would benefit from its power if they just gave it a chance. Regardless of what sickness you may have in this life, if practiced properly and rigorously, meditation will dramatically enhance your life. As a great Yogi master by the name of Lahiri Mahasaya once said, "meditate unceasingly!"

THIS IS the story of my awakening journey and how I discovered meditation and the spiritual realm in general. The summer of 2007 was only a blip in time...only a small part of my existence, but it was during this time that I was awakened to understand why my soul came here in the first place. For that, I will be forever grateful.

I wanted to share my story in order to make this experience more personal. I wanted you to understand that I am not some meditation or spiritual guru who believes he is better than you or knows more than you. Truthfully, I come from humble beginnings and am not proud of my past. In my life, I have done a lot of stupid things. I did not grow up in the best neighborhood, and our family had many problems, leaving me exposed to far too much when I was a child. That is simply the truth.

On the other hand, I would not change a single thing I have been through in life because those things have provided me with the thick skin I needed in order to make it. That includes all the experiences and all the people with whom I have come into contact. It is with genuine feeling that I can say I am thankful for everything on the spectrum.

I want you to know that the way I feel about these things is the way I hope you will be able to feel about your own awakening. There is a reason that you are going through what you did or are going through right now. It is okay if you cannot see it for what it is yet. You will look back on this time in the near future and understand why things happened the way they did. That is just the way life is, man.

It takes time for everything to heal. Before you can extract wisdom from an experience, you must fully integrate it. You must first go through it before you can look back and understand the whys, wheres, and hows.

The path to becoming the ultimate human begins with your awakening, no matter how old you are at the time. Some people awaken at the age of ten, others at the age of twenty, still others at the age of thirty, and still others at the age of fifty or more. Spiritually, it does not matter when you awaken for your journey. What is important is that you woke up.

There are people on this planet who live their entire lives and then die, never waking up, having to return and live another life before they finally get it right, before they finally experience their awakening.

So, congratulations on going through your awakening. This is the life in which your soul has finally chosen to awaken, and you will begin your journey to become the ultimate human, no matter how many lifetimes it takes. At the very least, you are on your way.

I want to take this chance to tell those of you who had your awakening a long time ago that I love, respect, and am grateful for you. You have now found yourselves in a position to more ably cope with all of the cosmic awareness you have been forced to integrate over the last few years or decades of your life. You can find the kind of routine and ritual that works for you, putting in the shadow work required to elevate your consciousness. (Learn about shadow work in Chapter 3).

You have learned how to use your newfound conscious awareness to create and bring about the life you really want to live. When you become super conscious and aware of the spirit realm, among other things, you will realize that this is not an easy thing to do.

There are many people who are the outcasts of their families, who are mocked, teased, and called crazy. They often have fragile psyches that cannot withstand the pressure that narrow-minded opinions and viewpoints put on them. They will either go back to the way they used to think and act or they will fall into depression.

Avoiding these dangers and making the most of your

awakening so that you can become more in tune with your frequency earns you my highest praise, highest regard, and deepest gratitude. For those of you who have not gotten there yet, know that we are all on our own path, at our own pace, and we will all get there eventually, to become the ultimate human.

My intentions are to see you all elevated in your lives! Let us travel home in love and oneness.

Musical Vibes for this chapter
Search: **CrewZ - My Best**
https://song.link/us/i/1465340401

First, love yourself

FLY

WHEN WE START GOING through our awakening and get into the thick of it, we realize that somewhere along the way we have lost touch with loving ourselves, loving who we are, and loving what we stand for. Many of us believe we love ourselves and may say, "I love myself," but in all honesty, if you are truthful with yourself, you will realize that you do not.

I do not want to generalize like that because I know there are plenty of people out there who practice self-love. I am speaking to those of you who either do not realize it yet or are well aware that you do not love yourself.

You do not look after yourself; you do not look after your health; you do not eat the right foods for your body; you do not exercise regularly; and you do not pamper yourself. Many years of not caring for oneself can lead to self-destruction of the body, health, and mind. As you begin to embark on the spiritual journey, you must learn to love yourself. They go hand in hand.

You will realize at some point during your awakening

process that you must completely love everything that is you because no one will ever love you more than you can love yourself. You must take care of your body, mind, and spirit in order to function smoothly in this reality. You need to be healthy and strong enough to go about your daily activities and act on your passion. To live to your fullest potential, you must have a healthy body.

Health equals wealth. As a result, self-love is everything.

A simple way to get started on the path to self-love is to come up with a few positive affirmations to say to yourself. Make a list of affirmations and read them aloud, one sentence at a time, word for word. If you can do it while looking at yourself in the mirror, that is even better.

You want to speak these words with a powerful conviction, with authority, and with the certainty that you will bring into existence whatever it is that you are declaring. Words generate vibrations. Words have tremendous power, and they speak your life into existence.

Because of this, you should always be very careful about the words you use, how you say things, and how you express yourself. Many of us speak in self-defeating ways without even realizing it. How many times did you tell yourself as a child, "Oh, I'm so stupid. I'm such an idiot." or "Man, why do I always do this? Why do I always make mistakes? Why do I always forget about this?"

Negative self-talk leads to a loss of self-love. Some of you cannot even look at yourself in the mirror at times. You are embarrassed by what you see, or you do not like who you see, or you do not like who you have become. It is okay to have these feelings. That is fine. It is something that many of us experience; no one is perfect. We all have features of ourselves and our bodies that we dislike or wish we could change.

To start loving yourself, look in the mirror in all of your glory and accept who you are. Accept your appearance and be content with it. Recognize that you are more than your body and face. You are a beautiful, immortal, infinite, and eternal being of light who is temporarily living as a human so that you can learn what it's like to be physical.

Keep in mind that you are a spiritual being first and a human being second. Do not get too caught up in your human life, your human body, or how you appear. Recognize that you are beautiful, regardless of how you may appear in the mirror. You are a magnificent being of pure light and power. Claim, own, and recognize this for what it is because it is your true essence.

I would like you to make a list for yourself.

Begin this list by telling yourself positive things to lift your spirits. "I am amazing at everything I do," for example. Recite this narrative to yourself: "I am beautiful. In my life, I always seem to attract the best possible scenarios. I am constantly attracting financial success opportunities. My life is under my control. I speak my life into being. My life is entirely in my hands. I will always be the best version of myself. I am always at my peak."

You must say these things and believe what you say. It is not just a belief; it is true. You must believe it, just as you believe the sky is blue. When it comes to manifesting for yourself, you need to speak your life into existence with confidence, knowledge, and faith in yourself.

This is the only way to bring about the changes you want in your life. You believe the sky is blue, right? Just as you believe the sky is blue, you believe that no one can deny that the sky is blue. You have known it your entire life. You already know it is blue. Nobody can tell you that it is yellow, green, or red.

The sky is blue. That is all there is to it. You already know this; no one can tell you otherwise.

Just like you know the blueness of the sky with zero degree of doubt, that is how much you need to believe in your manifestation, in your affirmation, and in what you are claiming to experience.

When you speak with confidence and without hesitation or doubt, you will learn how to bring what you want into your life on purpose. But it all starts with self-love. How can anyone else love you if you do not love yourself?

I am aware of a wonderful book written by Louise Hay titled *Mirror Work* that has been of great help to someone who is very close to me. I have seen the positive effects that this book has had on this individual. I believe the powerful message the book carries can definitely help and uplift many of you who may be in desperate need of reconnecting with yourself.

A conscious creator must have self-love and self-confidence. I recommend this wonderful self-love exercise that involves writing a love letter to yourself. In this love letter, you are describing everything you like about yourself or want to like about yourself. Maybe you feel like you cannot do something like this right now, but then something inside you says, "You know what? This is what I wish to become. I'd like to be able to do this."

I encourage you to follow the voice within and commit to making positive things happen. As such, begin speaking as if you have already done this in the present moment, and say things about yourself that you admire.

Write it down. Speak to yourself in the first person, writing down everything you like about yourself, all of your amazing qualities, everything you know you're good at: your talents, natural gifts, hobbies, what you want to be good at —everything.

Confidently write these things down for yourself; you will be surprised at what happens. You may well cry. You might laugh, or you might get stuck and think, "Man, I'm not sure. I do not like anything about myself. I really have very low self-esteem," or "I've been a mess or a screw up my entire life, and everything I touch turns out bad and blah, blah, blah." Your inner questioning turns into self-pity, and you are making yourself a victim.

You have to realize that those of you who think this way deserve to be loved and deserve to love yourself. You are deserving of this love.

Understand, guys, that self-love and self-worth go hand in hand. You must believe that you are worthy, because the fact that you are alive right now proves that you are worthy of life itself. You are worthy of being born. Do you understand how tough it is to take on a life on Earth!? Only the toughest of souls have the balls to be here in human form during such transformational times. That should say something about your strength and power you know nothing about yet. The fact that you are alive right now proves that you are valuable enough to be given life. You have always existed and will never cease to exist if you exist now. You are an immortal being outside of this body.

Take heart and relax, knowing that there is no rush in life. You have plenty of time to master your gifts, what you choose to act on, and what brings you the most joy and excitement in life. As you continue to do these wonderful things, you will find yourself loving yourself again.

The only way to love yourself is to let yourself be seen for who you really are. It is my firm conviction that meditation will help you with this.

Meditation helps people get in touch with their true consciousness and see the beauty of the divine spark of unconditional love and *Spirit* that is at their core. Once you see yourself in this light, you will never be able to unsee it. As a result, you will always be aware of how beautiful and magnificent you are, as well as how beautiful and magnificent everyone else is.

It is simply a matter of remembering that we are all *Spirit* and magnificent beings of light. After we have fully remembered and integrated this knowledge, it is our duty and responsibility to share it with anyone who will listen. Everything starts with self-love. Love yourself because you are the most magnificent work of art you have ever created.

Musical Vibes for this chapter

Search: <u>**CrewZ - Reflections**</u>

https://song.link/us/i/1382468147

Shadow Work

TO PROGRESS SUCCESSFULLY in your spiritual journey, you must be willing to face the challenges presented by the process called "shadow work." Shadow work is the effort an individual must do in order to search the subconscious mind in order to find those ideas that we hide or suppress and are considered by ourselves to be undesirable traits.

This important work has many benefits, but one of the main reasons for identifying and confronting these repressed ideas and traits is how it benefits others. Very often, we punish others around us who display these traits—traits that are locked within ourselves and ones we refuse to deal with. It is crucial to our own health and happiness that we do this shadow work in an effort to expunge these negative aspects that we see in ourselves and that we attribute to others simply because we have not cleaned out our own house.

As you progress along the path to becoming the ultimate human, you will come to the realization that there is a significant amount of shadow work that needs to be completed.

There are a lot of things from your past that you need to bring back to the forefront of your conscious mind.

One of the most difficult aspects of spiritual awakening is doing shadow work. Admitting to yourself that you are messed up or have problems you are not solving is a sobering process. For many people, being honest with themselves is extremely difficult. Many of us are so good at creating a false image of ourselves that it can be too painful to look at when we start to finally peel back the layers and start exposing our true selves again. You have to do shadow work if you want to make progress in the parts of your life that have to do with healing and waking up.

The hardest part about doing shadow work is being completely honest with yourself. There can be no biased perspectives, no attempts to exaggerate things, and no attempts to exaggerate yourself.

You must be honest and authentic with yourself, admitting your flaws, admitting that you need help, and admitting that you need to improve in certain areas of your life. You must be willing to look back at your childhood, revisit all of your traumas and dysfunctional behaviors, and understand what caused them.

To figure out how and why you were able to go through or do these things, you need to understand your current level of awareness and remember who you were in the past. You are extracting meaning from within when you review these things. When you extract meaning from your experiences, you gain intelligence and wisdom. That, in my opinion, is true intelligence.

This way of getting smarter is a natural part of evolution because you do not need books, videos, teachers, instructors, or mentors to do it. It is just you and your thoughts.

You are deriving meaning from within and learning from your experience. My friends, that is a lovely way to gain knowledge.

Many of us are afraid of doing shadow work because we are afraid of the emotions that will arise. This is why we keep it bottled up in the first place. We do not want to confront our feelings. We do not want to confront our emotions, particularly as men. Many men, for example, find it difficult to be emotional, cry, or be vulnerable about how they feel because they have been programmed to believe that doing so indicates weakness.

Emotions are synonymous with weakness, and sensitivity is synonymous with weakness. They bottle up those emotions and deal with them later, but they never end up dealing with them because they grow inside of them, creating internal anger, frustration, a quick temper, and impatience, all the while wondering where such negative traits came from.

All of this, however, stems from our refusal to confront our emotions. Doing shadow work is very important if you want to move forward in the process of spiritual growth you are going through.

You must be honest with yourself, and you must choose to want to heal yourself, your behaviors, and your traumas. Even if you were the one who caused trauma for others, you must forgive yourself, relive those experiences, and understand why you were able to hurt that person.

You must be willing to understand and accept painful situations where you may have been the one hurt. You must be able to see that experience from the perspective of everyone involved. In learning how to be empathic enough to understand everybody's perspective and everyone's dysfunctional behavior, you have to become one with all that is.

The challenge is to become one with your entire experience, your entire memory. When you can do this, you will be able to put yourself in the shoes of everyone involved in your traumatic past memory and thus understand why a person is capable of doing unwanted or unexpected things. The level of awareness from which a person is capable of doing what they have done is determined by the level of awareness from which their core being operates.

If their core being has a low frequency, you will understand how they can commit such crimes or cause you or your loved ones so much pain.

Becoming one with your entire experience makes it easier for you to forgive those who have hurt you in the past. In order to have the strength to do so, you need to gain some empathy. This clarity in your life will come from your shadow work. It will also release any pressure you may be feeling on your shoulders or anything within you that has been holding you back.

The more shadow work you do, the more you will be able to move forward and make progress in your life. You cannot get away from your own shadow.

The truth is, and this is the reality, that we have shadows in this realm. We are currently in third density as we transition into fourth density. (Chapter 4 discusses densities). However, as long as we remain in third density, shadows are real and do exist.

You cannot get away from your shadow.

When you walk down the street with the sun shining on you, your shadow follows you around the entire time. It is unavoidable. Accept your shadow, your darkness, your trauma, and your emotional injuries. You must accept every-thing that is not in harmonic vibration with your beingness. Accept it for what it is. See it for what it is and make the decision to let go of things that no longer serve you.

The more you begin to cleanse your auric field, the more alive you will feel in your practice, in your daily life, and in all of your actions. You will begin to formulate solutions to your problems and issues. As you move forward, you will start to vibrate at a higher frequency. As you do this, you will gain more wisdom, knowledge, and experience.

Because we do not live in a perfect world and because we are not perfect beings, shadow work will continue to happen until you are fully in fourth density.

Even then, who knows what new challenges await us?

Shadow work is a continuous process in our lives that we must maintain. We need to keep healing ourselves and shedding anything that no longer serves us so that we can realize our greatest potential.

The goal is to be a fully integrated man or woman. It is, without a doubt, a personal goal of mine. I hope that it is a new goal for you guys, if it is not an existing goal already, because you are all on the path to becoming the ultimate human.

I would like you to close your eyes and imagine yourself. Consider the version of yourself that is completely healed: a life healed of all your traumas, suffering, and pain, as well as everything you have hidden inside and are ashamed of.

Imagine the best, healed version of yourself right now.

Do you recognize that version of yourself? If you cannot, it is fine. But I strongly encourage you to try. Begin with the smallest aspects of your healing. Consider the following scenario: You have a paper cut. Start picturing that paper cut healing, the skin healing itself over time, and you healing yourself. Then you begin to work your way up higher. Start picturing yourself being healed from that traumatic event you went through as a child, or seeing yourself as completely healed and no longer affected by old memories, emotions, or behaviors.

Visualize the version of yourself that is happy, healed, and fulfilled. Did you know that the version of yourself you see in your mind's eye is actually existing and operating somewhere in some parallel reality, the universe, or somewhere in creation?

That person you identify as yourself exists in reality at this very moment, and you can become that person at will. That is how powerful you are when you learn and implement the right steps toward becoming the ultimate human.

With time, you will make that version of yourself a reality by taking action toward healing, making the conscious choice and decision to heal, and having the intention to heal. How quickly this happens for you depends on how strongly, passionately, and driven you are to become that version of yourself.

You can do this. You have already been healed. Speak as if the event has already occurred. You must let go of all "what ifs" and replace them with "as ifs," then insert the positive behavior or experience.

Remember that you are a being who speaks life into existence. We attach words, thoughts, emotions, and beliefs to our intentions. Shadow work is a mental and emotional practice that will help everyone in the long run, as long as it is put into practice and steps are taken to help you grow and heal, accept yourself, and love yourself. Continue to work with your shadow, love it, and see all the glory that is in you!

Allow love to command your ego and your shadow, and you will see that, over time, a whole new version of you will emerge from all of your efforts to become the ultimate human.

Musical Vibes for this chapter
Search: **CrewZ - So Much Heart**
https://song.link/us/i/1586568882

Densities

THERE WILL COME a time when you will eventually come across the realization that there are many layers within existence that we refer to as densities and dimensions. Many people around the world are starting to wake up to the truth of multidimensionality, parallel realities, and moving through realities.

A lot of us do not fully comprehend what densities are when we first encounter them.

What does this topic have to do with becoming the ultimate human? A big part of understanding your true nature is to realize that consciousness is multidimensional. This means you are existing in multiple dimensional levels of existence simultaneously to this very reality you currently find yourself in.

When you wake up every morning, you are only tuned into this one reality. But when you are in REM sleep or in deep meditation, you once again are operating from the multidimensional self more naturally. While we unconsciously roam amongst our multidimensional selves throughout our sleep, we don't usually retain the memories of these experiences very well. However, through meditation, we operate from this level consciously, and we can retain every aspect of the experiences.

THE TERM "DENSITY" delineates the level of consciousness within a particular essence of existence. There are seven levels of densities. These definitions can be found in the primary resources of the Law of One Ra Material (1989) and the Cassiopeia Transcripts (1994).

There are seven distinct levels, beginning with the First Density, which includes the most basic elemental essences of life, such as molecules and their subatomic particles. From the first level, you continue to ascend all the way to the Seventh Level, which is the extinction of individuality as we merge into unity consciousness with the Creator or God itself.

You can compare densities to the chakra system within humans. The seven chakras within your spine from the base to the top of your head, are a smaller version of the seven layers of existence that can be experienced.

We are in Third density, which represents the realm of duality. The solar plexus realm is where you still contain all the qualities of the first and second chakras. (Survival instinct, fight or flight, emotions, sexual energy, etc.)

It is the Third and Fourth Densities that affect the spiritual journey of humans most often. Fourth Density represents the Heart Chakra, where souls now find their heart centers opening, once again exposing them to the oneness in all Life. Through this oneness, we begin to understand unconditional love again and realize that truly, we are all one consciousness experiencing ourselves subjectively.

The beginnings of human self-awareness are found in Third Density. Third Density is bound by the constructs of time as we know it and three-dimensional space. Every level moves from and to other levels progressively and via natural evolution.

Unfortunately, most people are locked mentally and vibrationally in the confines of the Third Density. It is within the Third Density that people begin to develop a sense of consciousness that allows them to interact with others both negatively and positively.

People can get closer to breaking through the barriers between Third and Fourth Density as they grow spiritually. We can move back and forth and go beyond the limits of Third Density. People are not necessarily bound by the laws of physicality, and they learn this when they begin to further expand their consciousness.

Fourth Density allows people to grow spiritually to higher degrees, enabling them to achieve supernatural abilities such as telepathy, astral projection, channeling, instant manifestation, and much more. In Fourth Density, people can move back and forth between the physical and the ethereal and are not bound by linear time. This means you can shift from the present to the past or the future at will. Fourth Density beings are quasi-physical, meaning their half physical half etheric beings. They can easily phase shift between both realms.

Fifth Density serves as a place for beings to rest in ethereal existence before ascending higher. Here we do not take a physical body. Sixth Density serves as a place outside time and space for beings of pure energy. It is said that our higher self, which is your oversoul that is having all the simultaneous lifetimes to this one, resides in Sixth Density. These densities are meant to be evolutionary steps for souls to go through on their way to the Seventh Density, where we merge back with the Creator.

For people in our time in this world, ascending into Fourth Density is the most important goal of a person's spiritual journey. Sticking around in Third Density, where growth cannot go beyond the limits of time and space, is not good for a person's spiritual growth unless they wish to keep relearning life lessons within this dualistic realm.

To each his own.

HOW DOES density compare to dimension in the context of our spiritual journey?

That is where confusion can exist. We might say that a Third or Fourth-Density being or person is the same as a third or fourth-dimensional being. This would be easy to understand if we understood that most people are forced to live within the limits that three-dimensional space gives them. And if we are referring to Fourth Density beings, it makes sense to say that they live in a fourth dimension of space.

When trying to figure out how the terms have anything to do with improving the growth of our spiritual conscious-ness, they are very vague.

The most important thing to know is that people can thrive while working on a spiritual path that helps them move from one level of density and dimension to the next. Each step forward is important for the development of human consciousness. And that path becomes possible by integrating things like the power of meditation and Kriya Yoga into our journey.

Musical Vibes for this chapter

Search: <u>**CrewZ - 4th Density**</u>

https://song.link/us/i/1382467759

Paramahansa Yogananda

ONE OF THE most important yogis who ever lived wrote a most effective spiritual transformation book in 1946. In 1920, Yogananda, an immensely powerful yogi, moved from India to the United States. This man did what no other Indian yogi has ever done. He succeeded in giving free lectures all across the American continent at a time when the majority of people in the United States were closed-minded to anything other than Christianity.

By demonstrating how yoga, religion, and spirituality are all intertwined with one another, Yogananda was able to win over the hearts of the people living in America. Because of the positive way in which he discussed Jesus Christ, people paid attention to what he had to say.

Yogananda gave thousands of talks during this time, during which he taught the science of Kriya Yoga. He told his audiences about its inner workings and what it was supposed to do. The sage Babaji, who is also called the deathless guru, is said to have brought Kriya Yoga, a very powerful science and type of meditation, back to the forefront of Hindu philosophy in the 1800s, via his direct disciple Lahiri Mahasaya. Kriya Yoga is a method of yoga that purports to be able to circumvent death.

Yogananda stemmed from a long line of powerful yogis and gurus who could do amazing things, displaying powers that were beyond human. For a decade (1910-1920), Yogananda trained and lived with his guru, Sri Yukteswar, an astrologer in India, in his hermitage, where he learned many things that would assist him in his life's journey and purpose in America.

Yogananda's purpose in life was to teach Kriya Yoga and meditation to people in the West. Before he did this, these practices were almost unknown in western societies.

Since 2007, I have been on a spiritual enlightenment journey. Before I learned about the book *Autobiography of a Yogi* by Paramahansa Yogananda, I thought I knew all about the spiritual realm. I thought this way because I felt I had already been exposed to so much through my own meditations and personal experiences. Although I believed I was very conscious about the spiritual world, I did not understand as much as I thought I did until I was exposed to this classic.

Fifteen years prior to the pandemic in 2005, I had first heard about Yogananda and his Autobiography. However, at that point in my spiritual development, I was nowhere near ready for what I would eventually learn and read. So, naturally, it didn't catch my attention yet. Then, in 2020, a good friend of mine brought it to my attention again. I seized upon the chance to listen to the audio version during the COVID quarantine that summer. Since the audiobook has almost eighteen hours of recordings, I thought it would be a perfect companion during the long days of the pandemic.

Once I started, I could not stop listening. I finished it in a week and a half and felt it had changed my life forever.

Becoming the Ultimate Human was inspired by the powerful testimony of Yogananda's life.

Yogananda's teachings on Kriya Yoga and the miracles he saw firsthand during his life made me want to find and reach deeper levels of the human experience. This led to my preoccupation with achieving the ultimate human form. I became intrigued with this topic because of Yogananda's yogi lineage. I wanted to know all about the mysteries of human potential.

Since childhood, I have dreamed that I possess psychic and spiritual skills. Yogananda's book is probably the best thing that's ever happened to me. It reawakened a new spark of curiosity in my spiritual development. I am happy to include all of this information in this book for you. I highly suggest that you purchase a copy of *Autobiography of a Yogi*, even if you have never heard of it. May the words you are reading right now serve as confirmation that it is time to read this book.

I believe that this book is a critical-read for anyone who wants to find spiritual enlightenment or grow to their fullest potential. You cannot live a conscious lifestyle without knowing who Yogananda is and what his lifetime of work has brought to the evolution of humanity's consciousness into Fourth density.

As I mentioned before, Kriya Yoga is a very powerful ancient science that was brought back in the nineteenth century by the deathless guru, Babaji. Lahiri Mahasaya, who was his direct disciple, was taught the main ideas of this philosophy. Then he told him to teach the tens of thousands of followers he would gather all over India.

There is a lot of old knowledge in these teachings about how a person can achieve god-consciousness while still living in a human body. In his book, *Autobiography of a Yogi*, Yogananda says that it takes a person one million disease-free years for their brain to develop enough to be able to handle the power that is needed to be in full god-consciousness.

Obviously, none of us are capable of living one million years in one human body. So, yogis came up with a way to get a million years of spiritual brain development in just one lifetime. Call it a shortcut or a loophole.

In order to achieve a million years of natural and spiritual evolution in the brain, Yogananda says one needs to practice the Kriya Yoga meditations for eight and a half hours per day, every day for three years. If one does Kriya Yoga for eight and a half hours every day, it is akin to having achieved 1,000 years of natural and spiritual development in the brain.

So, if this schedule were followed carefully for an entire year, it would be like getting an extra 365,000 years of natural evolution. This means that after three years of such effort, a person would have the equivalent of a million years of real god-consciousness.

Now, I know some of you reading this may be thinking, "How can I possibly do Kriya Yoga meditation for eight and a half hours a day if I need to sleep?" Well, it appears that these yogis learned to do Kriya Yoga meditation instead of sleeping.

The human body gets an abundant, unlimited amount of cosmic energy when under the meditative state of being, but only a small amount of cosmic energy when it is in REM sleep every night. I could see why it would be possible to be able to meditate or do Kriya Yoga meditation for eight and a half hours a day. Of course, this is something these yogis have dedicated their entire lives to. No beginner yogi is ever going to be able to do Kriya Yoga for eight and a half hours at the beginning of their spiritual journey.

This is something that takes years of practice after being initiated into Kriya Yoga. A Kriyaban must teach you how to do real Kriya Yoga before you can learn it. A Kriyaban is a dedicated student and teacher of Kriya Yoga. It is said that Yogananda personally initiated 100,000 human beings into kriya yoga in his lifetime!

Yogananda founded the Self-Realization Fellowship (SRF) so that anyone from anywhere in the world could learn the true teachings of Kriya Yoga. Kriyananda was one of Yogananda's direct disciples. Kriyananda also set up a network of Ananda centers around the world where people might learn Kriya Yoga. Both of these groups are well-known and official ways to get started with Kriya Yoga.

I encourage you to do some research to find a group in your region.

Initiation into Kriya Yoga is not open to everyone. One must show that they care about why this path is important and explain in detail why they want to study Kriya Yoga, meditation, and science.

Once a person joins one of these groups, they will have to go through a series of procedures before being introduced to Kriya Yoga. This gets the students' minds ready for all the information they need to know to start Kriya Yoga.

For these spiritual leaders, nothing compares to the bond shared between a guru and his student. The real job of a guru is to teach his students the spiritual practices and training that will help them become the best versions of themselves to where an external guru is no longer needed.

It is important to follow the lineage of Paramahansa Yogananda's famous teachers to find out where he learned his wisdom. Sri Yukteswar's job was to prepare Yogananda for bringing the science of Kriya Yoga and meditation to the West. This would show people in the West that there is more than one way to understand God, spirituality, and the mysteries of the world. Sri Yukteswar was just one of the many thousands of people who learned from Lahiri Mahasaya, also a powerful guru.

Even though he was just one among thousands of Lahiri Mahasaya's students, Yukteswar had reached a highly advanced level of practice. Yukteswar spent his entire life working toward this goal, and as a result, he became a very powerful avatar.

Yogananda's parents also learned from Lahiri Mahasaya firsthand. There is a powerful story in the Autobiography *of a Yogi* that explains how Yogananda's father chose to become a direct disciple of Lahiri Mahasaya, which I will leave for you guys to discover after you finish my book. The purpose of Mahasaya's life was to reintroduce the science of Kriya Yoga to as many people as possible. This is how he was able to gain thousands of followers in India and, later, all over the world.

His goal in sharing this knowledge was to help people rediscover and return to the path that leads to true fourth-density consciousness and beyond through the power of the breath. According to Yogananda, when the brain, spinal column, and central nervous system are all connected in this way, a person's consciousness can finally meet the conscious universe. Anyone who does Kriya Yoga or any other method that helps this link between the brain, spinal cord, and central nervous system will reach God.

Lahiri Mahasaya was taught by the immortal master Babaji. Babaji is known as the "deathless guru" because he is an immortalized *Spirit* who lives in the body of what looks like a twenty-five-year-old man who never ages. Yogananda describes Babaji to having long, copper-colored hair and that he often shows up with or without a beard or mustache. In order that people might see what Babaji looked like, Yogananda described these details to an artist during his lifetime.

In Chapter 33 of Yogananda's autobiography, we learn about Babaji, the modern-day "Yogi-Christ" of India. It serves as a good introduction to this important yogi. Yogananda is sure that Babaji's mission is to live through the ages and help people become more aware of God.

Since this is the case, it is thought that Babaji will stay in his youthful form until the end of this yuga cycle (a cyclic age in Hindu cosmology that lasts 4.32 million years), continuing to help and guide people. This will bring believers one step closer to their ultimate spiritual and communal goal.

So far, I have talked about three great Indian yogis: Sri Yukteswar, Lahiri Mahasaya, and Mahavatar Babaji. Yukteswar, Lahiri Mahasaya, and Babaji were not your average Indian gurus. Extraordinary skills and their connection to the divine allowed these men of Earth to transform their fleshy bodies into orbs of light, soar into the clouds, and return to Earth in full human form.

They were able to be in two locations at once, which gave them incredible strength and flexibility. They have many other powers that I will not reveal here because I want you to discover them on your own as you read the *Autobiography of a Yogi*. Yet, I believe that the book is magical enough to keep you reading, thinking, wondering, and wanting more.

I hope to follow in the footsteps of these great yogis by becoming a Kriya Yoga initiate and succeeding in the same way they did. My greatest aspiration is to become the best human I can be in this life and reach a million years of natural spiritual growth in three years. At some point during my life, I hope to devote three years to this discipline. I do not know when this will be or how old I will be when I do this, but I do know that it is my path.

Numerous influential figures, including Steve Jobs, can trace their inspiration to Yogananda. It is widely known that every year until the day he died, Jobs read the *Autobiography of a Yogi*. Steve Jobs also made sure that everyone who attended his burial received a copy of this book as they left the service. This was the only book he ever stored on his personal iPad.

Since Yogananda left the earth, the story of his life has had a life-altering impact on a significant number of people who, in turn, have gone on to make great changes in the world.

Yogananda's exit from this world was inspirational. On March 7, 1952, he addressed a crowd of over six hundred people in Los Angeles, California. During his speech, he expressed his admiration for the United States and India and called for closer ties between the two superpowers.

At the end of his speech, he read a short version of one of his many poems. In his final moments, his last words were, "I am hollowed. My body has touched the sod." It is said that he let out a long sigh with that word, sod. In that instance, he collapsed in front of everyone, never to return to his body.

While speaking to a large crowd of people, Yogananda attained Mahasamadhi (also known as the Yogi's Great Exit). It is said that the bodies of people who reach Mahasamadhi will stay in good shape for up to thirty days after the yogi leaves. This means that their bodies will not start to decay or decompose for at least thirty days. In fact, this is precisely what occurred to Yogananda's physical form. It is said his body gave off the fragrance of flowers. As incredible as it may seem to people today, Yoganandya's body remained in excellent condition for weeks after his death. I find this story absolutely amazing.

I am grateful that this beautiful man chose to grace our earth in order to remind us of our true potential, teaching us how we can reach God-consciousness through Kriya Yoga.

Musical Vibes for this chapter
Search: **CrewZ - Inside**
https://song.link/us/i/1382467779

Mahasamadhi

THE YOGI'S Great Exit

To comprehend what Mahasamadhi is, we must first acknowledge that there are numerous stages that humans go through in order to first achieve Samadhi. Samadhi, according to Paramahansa Yogananda, is a soundless state of breathlessness.

Many people consider this blissful yoga experience to be the first rung on the ladder to enlightenment. This is the point at which a yogi finally discovers his or her true identity as an immortal *Spirit* and an integral part of the cosmos. In order for me to explain this properly, I will need to introduce you to Maharishi Patanjali and the significance of what his writings imply for those of us who choose to go on this journey.

Patanjali was a very brilliant man and the author of three known texts, but the most famous was The *Yoga Sutra*. In the *Yoga Sutra*, he proposes an eight-step process referred to as the Eight Limbs of Yoga. On the path to Samadhi, a yogi must perform and experience these eight steps in order to reach their goal.

The eighth and final step is referred to as samadhi. Samadhi is the spiritual and intellectual peak reached via meditation.

THE EIGHT LIMBS OF YOGA

Ashtanga Yoga refers to the traditional eight limbs of the yoga practice. Self-discipline, or *Yamas*, is the name given to the first of the eight limbs of yoga.

Niyama, which literally translates to "observance," is the second one.

Asana, or yoga postures and stances, is the third component of yoga and arguably the most well-known outside of India. The practice of *pranayama* teaches one to manage their breath.

Pratyahara is the restraint of the senses; *Dharana* is attention or concentration; *Dhyana* is meditation; and *Samadhi* is unification in ultimate consciousness, or mindlessness.

The Yamas, Niyamas, Asanas, and Pranayamas are the first four limbs of yoga, and they are the external aspects of yoga's eight limbs.

Pratyahara, Dharana, Dhyana, and Samadhi are the remaining four limbs of yoga, and they represent the internal aspects of the eight limbs of yoga and can be more difficult to attain.

A better understanding of the system can be attained by investigating each of the eight components in greater detail.

The **Yamas** come in at number one on the list. They are a set of ethical precepts that outline the correct way to live one's life. It is a rundown of activities or behaviors that should be avoided at all costs in this life.

These things should never be done if one is to live a decent life.

In the *Yoga Sutra*, there are five rules called Yamas. Here is an explanation of each one. The first is called Ahimsa or Ahinsa, and it translates to "nonviolence." The practice of Ahimsa is based on the idea that one should not think, say, or do anything that could be construed as harmful to other living beings.

The second precept is called Satya and refers to ultimate truth or honesty. This means being honest in one's thinking as well as in one's words and actions.

The third is known as Asteya or Acharya in Sanskrit, and it translates to "do not steal." Asteya is a moral doctrine in Hinduism that instructs followers to abstain from taking other people's possessions and to not even entertain the idea of appropriating another person's words, ideas, or actions. (It is comparable to the Judeo-Christian tenth command-ment to not covet thy neighbor's property).

The third yama is known as Brahmacharya. This is the discipline of leading an abstinence-free lifestyle and gaining mastery over one's body and mind through the practice of meditation.

Aparigraha, which literally translates to "non-greedi-ness," is the last of the yamas. The idea is to avoid becoming a service to self individual who gets what they want at the expense of others.

The **Niyamas**, often known as "positive observances or obligations," make up the second limb of yoga. The Niyamas are seen as the ethical behaviors that enable one to live a healthy life and attain spiritual enlightenment in the Yogic tradition.

Niyamas, much like Yamas, can be broken down into the five components listed here. Shaucha, which can be defined as purity and clearness of speech, body, and mind, is the first and most important quality.

Santosha, also known as contentment and satisfaction, is the second.

The third one is called tapas, and it is a spiritual practice that helps people achieve moksha, which is another word for emancipation. As a method of instilling self-discipline, tapas involves meditation and calls for periods of isolation.

The last is Ishvara Pranidhana. This signifies that in order to experience all, one must consecrate and surrender oneself to the Supreme God's absolute might.

Asanas are yoga's third limb. Most people think yoga is all about asanas. Many people have the wrong idea that yoga is only about getting into different poses of the body in order to gain more flexibility and strength, and this is not the case.

Asanas are agreeable body positions, according to Patanjali's *Yoga Sutra*. Asanas are introspective and meditative positions that can assist you in being motionless for extended periods of time. The whole purpose of doing asanas is to prepare the body to receive higher frequencies attracted during meditation. However, asanas are not required to attract these frequencies. Only observation of the breath and stillness of the mind is truly required

There are twelve asanas mentioned by the Sage Patanjali, which are:

- Padmasana

- Virasana
- Bhadrasana
- Svastikasana
- Dandasana
- Sopas Rasayana
- Paryankasana
- Krauncha-nishadasana
- Hastanishadasana
- Ushtranisha
- Samasthanasana
- Sthira Sukhasana

Pranayama is the name given to the fourth component of the yoga practice.

The term "Pranayama" originates from the Sanskrit "Prana," which may be translated as "breath" or "life-giving power," and "Ayama," which can mean "control" or "restraining." Therefore, pranayama could be referred to as, the regulation of the breath.

Patanjali elaborated further on the technique of pranayama, which is seen as an essential exercise for developing one's ability to focus.

Pratyahara is the name given to the fifth of the eight limbs of yoga. It is derived from two Sanskrit words: prate, which means away or anti, and ahara, which means nourishment or items that are mostly consumed externally. The removal of food and the senses is known as Pratyahara. This limb is actually one of the key limbs that connects the external limbs to the internal limbs of yoga, and it is referred to as the connecting limb.

Engaging in pratyahara assists anyone in achieving Dharana, Dhyana, and Samadhi if they can gain mastery over all of their senses and create the ideal environment for their own self-realization.

Dharana is the sixth limb of yoga, and its name refers to either having a single-minded concentration or the ability to maintain steadiness. This involves focusing one's attention on a single thing, such as a mantra or one's breath, in order to prevent the mind from wandering and shifting to thoughts that are not necessary.

Dharana is the beginning of the stage of deep focus that ultimately leads to meditation.

Dhyana is the name given to the seventh part of the yogic path, and it encompasses both meditation and introspection. Dhyana is the meditative practice one engages in that assists their mind to enter the meditative state of being.

Samadhi is the eighth and final limb of the yoga practice. Samadhi is the most accomplished state of yoga. This experience is reached when a person's mind attains complete stillness and is now experiencing their mind expand in blissful ways. More and more of this expansion leads to you integrating higher frequencies into your auric field. With time you will have an experience in cosmic consciousness.

STAGES OF SAMADHI

If you research the term "Samadhi," you will realize that there are many different types of Samadhis. For the sake of simplicity, we will be covering the two levels of Samadhi according to Patanjali's *Yoga Sutra*.

The first level of Samadhi is *Samprajnata* Samadhi, also known as *Savikalpa* Samadhi. You have reached a point in your meditation where there is utter stillness and calm. But you are still in touch with reality and can interact with it as usual. As you sit quietly, you consciously eliminate mental distractions while meditating.

Savikalpa Samadhi is known as a state of conditioned oneness. Here, the person who is meditating can feel his soul merge with infinite consciousness itself. Unfortunately, however, the meditator cannot preserve the experience outside of the actual meditation.

According to Patanjali, in Savikalpa Samadhi, you lose all human consciousness, but only for a short period of time. In this state, time and space are distinct from our linear world. Savikalpa Samadhi is not a permanent state, so everyone must eventually return to normal consciousness. Patanjali then describes the four stages of Savikalpa Samadhi, which can be experienced as well.

Savitarka Samadhi is the name given to the initial step of the Savikalpa Samadhi process. This can be translated to mean "thinking change or transformation upon an item by the use of words." It is the stage of learning information that helps us distinguish reality from illusion. Our ideas will become objects with the assistance of the words that we say, and this will initiate a conversation between the two of us.

The name of this exchange is *Tarka*.

In the meditative state known as Savitarka Samadhi, the mind applies its consciousness to evaluate whether or not a topic should be brought up for discussion.

Sa-asmita Samadhi is the second stage of Savikalpa Samadhi. It is important to note that Sa-asmita Samadhi is the conclusion of Savitarka Samadhi. At this stage, the yogi's mind has grown even more refined via sustained concentration on the breath or a single thought, allowing for greater insight into the nature of awareness as a whole.

Savichara Samadhi is stage three. Moving deeper into Savichara Samadhi, the yogi may grasp the nature of time and space. This may aid our comprehension of the cosmic consciousness. Savichara Samadhi is a state of silent, peaceful thinking.

Stage four of Savikalpa Samadhi is called *Sa-ananda* Samadhi. When a person reaches this stage of Savikalpa Samadhi, their mind transcends their intellect. When in this state, there is no logic; there is just a vacant and quiet mind. When you are in this state, your mind is so clear that it can only see the happiness it brings to itself.

Everything that I have mentioned so far about Samadhi, is only in reference to Savikalpa Samadhi.

The second level of Samadhi is *Asamprajnata* Samadhi, also known as *Nirvikalpa* Samadhi. When you attain Nirvikalpa Samadhi, you delve so far inside yourself that no outside stimulation affects you. The consciousness is marked by pure emptiness. A yogi who makes it through this phase has abandoned all attachments, gained discriminative intelligence, and refined their mental purity. Nirvikalpa is reported to have been experienced by Yogananda's master, Sri Yukteswar, Swami Vivekananda, and a few others.

Nirvikalpa Samadhi is divided into three stages. The initial level of samadhi is known as *Nirvitarka* Samadhi. Here, the mind becomes engrossed in one form and goes beyond the perspective of just being the knower or observer. In this experience, we have more power over the intellect, the mind, and its concepts.

Stage two is known as *Nirvichara* Samadhi. The mind has evolved to the point where it can transcend its own sense of time and place. At this very instant, the opportunity to achieve a genuine and undivided state of consciousness actually presents itself for the very first time.

Kaivalya Samadhi, the highest stage of Nirvikalpa Samadhi, represents the pinnacle of enlightenment. In this final phase, you will become one with eternal consciousness and permanently bonded to the ethers.

Numerous yogis and saints concur that a human being is capable of attaining a meditative state of being by maintaining focus on observing the breath for the duration of twelve breaths.

I had to tell you all of this about Samadhi and its different levels so that you could understand how important and powerful Mahasamadhi is. By now, you should have a better idea of the different phases the mind goes through as it goes deeper into itself to reach higher levels to operate from.

It is very important to integrate, study, and understand all of this information if you are embarking on the path of becoming the ultimate human. Understanding the different stages the mind goes through as we try to reach higher states of consciousness is a deep and complicated process. Every yogi or yogini on this path will benefit greatly from understanding this information.

MAHASAMADHI

The majority of people living on this planet have some type of fear associated with death. It makes no difference whether it is their own death or the death of someone they care about. Near the time of their passing, the vast majority of people are typically accompanied by some degree of terror. This is due to the fact that the majority of us do not have an adequate understanding of death or what lies beyond it.

People are wired to be afraid of things they do not comprehend, and this anxiety will never go away when it comes to the unknown region of death. If someone were to suggest to you, "Did you know that as a human being, you have the capacity to consciously leave your body whenever you so choose?" what would your response be?

ALTHOUGH THE VAST majority of people would consider or equate this with a form of suicide, Mahasamadhi is not the same thing. When a person makes the decision to end their own life, there is almost always some kind of physical injury that occurs to their body. It is possible that someone committed suicide by stabbing themselves, shooting themselves, poisoning themselves, or jumping off a cliff. No matter the circumstances, it invariably results in harm to the human body.

You leave the body when this happens.

Imagine for a moment that you had the ability to exit the body intentionally without having to inflict any harm on the body in the process. This is Mahasamadhi, also known as the Yogi's Great Exit or the Goal of Every Yogi.

The state of Mahasamadhi is often regarded as the ultimate goal of yoga practice. When a yogi reaches the point in their life where they feel that they have done, created, and experienced everything that they possibly could have in this particular lifetime, the yogi will make preparations to consciously exit the body, never to return.

There are many accounts of humans from all walks of life who have attained Mahasamadhi. They include not just

Paramahansa Yogananda but also every other yogi, master, and guru that came before him in his lineage.

Another, more recent, description of Mahasamadhi was recorded by a woman who went by the name Vijji and was the wife of Sadhguru.

Vijji was able to achieve Mahasamadhi by following the path of passion and devotion that she had shown towards her spouse, Sadhguru. This allowed her to succeed in her quest to achieve Mahasamadhi. Her husband was able to provide her with the direction she needed to achieve such a remarkable goal, even though she was still a young woman and the mother of a seven-year-old daughter at the time. And despite her young age, she was able to obtain it through enormous commitment. It was at this point in her life that she recognized her inner and outer beauty as being of equal value. People from all around showered her with love.

Even though she had lived a life full of honor and acclaim, she wished to end it through Mahasamadhi while things were still good. After intentionally training herself for a period of about eight months, she was finally able to achieve Mahasamadhi on January 23, 1997.

Vijji's husband is still a very well-known and influential yogi who gives people knowledge and wisdom and helps them get back on the path to the infinite.

Anyone sitting here right now reading this book has the ability to die mindfully through the practice of Mahasamadhi when their time on earth is up. Nobody should have to die as a result of disease, old age, or chance.

You have been taught to fear death despite the fact that you are the one who controls your life and may end it when-ever you choose. You have been conditioned to accept the certainty of death; you never know when it will strike, you cannot prevent it, and it is just something people cannot change, so you give in to that idea. And because you give in to that concept, you embrace the idea unequivocally that you are not immune to death from things like murder, accidents, sickness, and old age.

Which of the many roads leading to your destiny will you choose to travel now that you are aware of the possibilities that lie before you? It is possible that many of you who are reading this are thinking, "How can I achieve Mahasamadhi? What are the steps that must be taken for a person to reach such a state? What exactly is it that one needs to perform with their thoughts and their breath in order to even approach and accomplish Mahasamadhi?"

Mahasamadhi is a tremendous set of meditations and mental procedures that must be rigorously practiced. I have to admit that I do not yet fully comprehend the process. I feel in order to attain Mahasamadhi you must first be proficient in mastering Nirvikalpa Samadhi. To reach Nirvikalpa alone is no easy task, so it only makes sense that if you are to obtain Mahasamadhi, you must quite literally devote your entire being to that practice until it is achieved. This is why Mahasamadhi is something you would strive for towards the end of your life. As time goes on, it is my intention to exit this life by achieving Mahasamadhi. When the time comes, I will find a qualified yogi to help me.

At the end of one's life, reaching the state of Mahasamadhi is an achievement that I personally hope everyone achieves. Nobody deserves to die in a way that will have a detrimental effect on the people they love the most in the world. If a person were to choose the path of Mahasamadhi and pass away in this manner, I believe that rather than being mourned and missed by their family, they would be honored and respected, and it would be a much easier transition for anybody to accept when a loved one passes away.

MEDITATION IS the first step toward reaching Mahasamadhi, a state of consciousness that can only be reached by the human mind. Before any of us can make Mahasamadhi a reality for ourselves, we need to start at the very beginning of what it takes for human consciousness to reach this point. We start with meditation.

Musical Vibes for this chapter
Search: **CrewZ - Subconsciously Switching Flows**
https://song.link/us/i/1477891212

Meditation

~⁓~

MANY OF YOU reading this right now have already started or embarked upon your journey of meditation. On the other hand, many of you have never meditated a day in your life. However, if you are still reading at this point, then surely you must have some type of interest in learning how to meditate, or at the very least, understanding what meditation is and what it can do for us humans.

If you look up the word "meditation" in the dictionary, most definitions state that it means to think about something, to reflect, or to think about something religiously or spiritually with devotion.

Throughout my sixteen years of practicing meditation, I have come up with my own explanation that is based on my experience. Meditation is a spiritual practice that any human being can do, regardless of their beliefs or religious faith. Reaching a meditative state of being is achieved via an increased mental focus on the observation of the breath until the breath becomes almost nonexistent. At this point, the breath gets replaced by spiritual energy known also as cosmic energy. This entire process takes the conscious mind directly to the intelligent force behind your breath. That intelligence, which is animating your very breath, is what you are connecting to when you meditate. This is what I have found to be the process of meditation!

The whole point of meditation is to help a person reach the meditative state of being. As we attain this state more and more, we begin to gain benefits exponentially. The four main benefits of meditation are mental, physical, emotional, and spiritual.

When we are in a meditative state, we are in a different state of awareness and perception where we can access higher parts of ourselves. As a result, the more we expose our conscious mind to this state, the more in tune we will become with *Spirit* as well as our own consciousness. What is the key to achieving the meditative state of being? What must we humans do in order to get there?

The key to reaching this state is our breath.

Our breath is what gives us life; it is what animates the human body. If you can connect consciously to the intelligent force behind your breathing, you can connect directly to the divine spark of consciousness that you are. This part of you is the soul, that aspect of yourself that connects you to what people call "God."

Your breath is everything.

It is through the breath that we are capable of living life through the physicality of these human bodies. By noticing and becoming one with the natural inhalation and exhalation of our diaphragms, we can slowly move inward into our consciousnesses or minds, where we can start the process of experiencing the different samadhis.

It is here that we will start to move through our minds,

going deeper into ourselves via the breath. To reach higher states of consciousness, you need to work on developing your breath power and learning diaphragmatic breathing.

Most human beings today are breathing improperly. Most people breathe through their chests rather than through their lower abdomen, where the diaphragm is located. Many of us are breathing in a way that is known as survival mode. Survival mode breathing is when you are taking quick, short breaths without even realizing it.

Stress-induced breathing is caused by many years of stress, overthinking, anxiety, and a buildup of challenging experiences. These things will cause people to breathe in survival mode because we take in much less oxygen and start to create energetic blockages that stop cosmic energy from flowing through our bodies.

Over time, this energetic blockage will drain the body of cosmic energy, manifesting aches, pains, illness, and disease in the body. When a part of our body is energetically out of alignment, it will get sick because the energy flow is out of sync.

COSMIC ENERGY

Cosmic energy is known as a universal energy that exists all around us, 24/7. This is the energy that exists between planets, stars, and galaxies. It is omnipresent. This energy vibrates at a frequency beyond our field of perception, which is why most people cannot see cosmic energy.

Everyone, however, can feel cosmic energy if they focus and concentrate their minds sufficiently. This beautiful energy is what sustains light in our bodies. We need cosmic energy to operate in this realm. We receive a limited amount of cosmic energy every single night when we go to sleep. This is why, after a twelve to fifteen-hour day of daily activities, our bodies get depleted and exhausted and need to be replenished.

When we enter rapid eye movement (REM) sleep, our bodies are bathed in a cosmic energy shower, which is why we feel rejuvenated and ready to take on the day again after a good night's sleep. As I said previously, sleep only provides a limited amount of this energy, so we must sleep every night to replenish it.

When meditating intentionally, a person receives the same cosmic energy as during REM sleep. The difference is that we receive an unlimited, abundant amount of this energy when it is received via meditation. As you keep giving your body an endless supply of this energy, you will find yourself sleeping less and less over time. The more you meditate, the less you will find yourself sleeping. This is only true for people who are consistent with this practice.

As I mentioned earlier, cosmic energy is conscious of itself. It has its own intelligence. This intelligence knows where to go in the body that you need it most. Once this energy enters your body, it will constantly keep bombarding that area of the body.

If you meditate every day, cosmic energy will flow in abundance throughout your body every day. This can and will lead to miraculous healing in your body. With more and more cosmic energy flowing into the body, the body can heal itself over time.

How beautiful it is to know that there is an infinite source of energy that exists all around us, 24/7. It is an endless source of energy that we can pull straight out of the ethers by learning to control our breath.

Now, you see why the breath is very powerful, and it is essential for people to master the way that we breathe so that we can access higher states of consciousness.

WHAT YOU CAN EXPECT

What can we expect to happen if we get into a meditative state in our daily lives? What types of experiences can meditation bring? I wanted to include a few experiences that I have come to understand through my personal journey.

The beauty of meditation is that people never experience the same thing twice when entering the meditative state of being. It is always a brand new experience. This, in and of itself, makes meditation extremely enjoyable and exciting to practice because we get thrilled when we know we're going to experience something beneficial without knowing how it will happen.

It is exciting to venture into the unknown.

Next, during meditation, your body will be under a full shower of cosmic energy, as I mentioned before. During the whole experience, you may feel a deep sense of stability and security as you simultaneously feel a blissful and expansive sensation in your head region. Meditation will ground you to the earth in a sense where you feel in total connection with your body and with the cosmos.

Next, meditation will help you realize that you can become what is called the "Rainbow Bridge." You become the bridge between physical and spiritual matter. Remember your chakra system? Each chakra is related to a different color of the rainbow:

- The Root Chakra is red

- Sacral Chakra is orange
- Solar Plexus is yellow
- Heart Chakra is green
- Throat Chakra is blue
- Third Eye Chakra is indigo
- and the Crown Chakra is violet

The unique color layout of your chakra system makes you a literal rainbow bridge.

You are the vessel that connects the spirit world to the earthly realm. You are the vessel that anchors the cosmic energies of the universe onto the earth. This planet rises in frequency through every meditator.

You will also gradually realize that you are more than just your body as you practice getting into a meditative state of being. You are not limited by your physical body; there is far more to your total consciousness than just the human form. There are many layers in the auric field, and you will quickly realize this through meditation.

Meditation will also raise the frequency of your intelligence.

As we mentioned earlier in this book, your mind is a field of energy that is conscious of itself. This field of energy vibrates at a specific frequency. Whether or not you can understand something and how much intelligence you can express depends on what frequency your mind is vibrating at.

Your body and mind are receiving a shower of cosmic energy when you are in a meditative state. This energy will raise the vibration or frequency of your mind, which will help you reach higher levels of intelligence.

Meditation will also cause pineal gland activation. For

those of you who do not know what the pineal gland is, it is a gland at the center of every human brain on planet earth. Every human being has this gland in the center of their brains.

This gland contains rods, cones, and photoreceptors just as your two physical eyes do, making it a third eye. I like to refer to the pineal gland as the first eye because the brain and heart are the first organs to develop in the womb, before the eyes. Because the pineal gland is visible, it is your first and spiritual eye. This is the gland that helps people see into the inner worlds of light. It helps us see into the astral realities that exist within all of us.

Pineal gland activation enables people to access greater spiritual vision. Everyone has spiritual vision to a certain degree, and the more we build up this ability, the more we will be able to see with the spiritual eye.

Last but not least, you may also experience what is called an "out-of-body experience," also known as an astral projection. From my experiences with astral projection, I have personally concluded that it only seems to happen to individuals who manage to stay in this thoughtless state for extended periods of time.

While in this state cosmic energy is circulating throughout your body and after a while, this energy will continuously fill up your entire body. You will feel this energy and sometimes it's accompanied by light static sounds.

Eventually, you begin to feel a rush of energy in the spine as you simultaneously notice all of the energy within you culminating to a singular point in your body. This point is different for everyone, but for my first time ever it culminated in the front right side of my head before I heard a loud jar popping sound, projecting me into an instant sensation of boundlessness.

The rush of this energy can be overwhelming at first, before projecting. But if you let go of fear and allow the experience to occur, it will.

I was nineteen years old when this first happened to me in 2008, and it's a sensation one could never forget. I have had a bunch more since then but you will never forget your first.

When you have an out-of-body experience, you are no longer bound by the laws of normal reality. You have the ability to travel through matter. You are not affected by any of the four elements, so you can go anywhere in space and time. You are freed from the confines of time in a linear progression. You will meet and see other beings. When you are consciously operating within the astral template of reality, your thoughts will come into being right away.

Before attempting an astral projection, it is crucial for a person to have a firm grasp on their thoughts and emotions and be able to keep them in check at all times.

Without control, one may be exposed to a horrific experience.

You manifest instantaneously whilst in this realm. There is no delay like there is in Third density reality. You are responsible for what you create and experience. Your frequency of perception and how much you understand about the nature of reality will determine what you experience.

If you know you are a fearful person, you should not be attempting astral projection. It's best you first focus on elevating your mental state and strengthening your central nervous system via more and more meditation.

Now, astral projection is not the main focus of meditation and truly isn't of much importance when it comes to the journey of your self-realization back to the Divine. It's merely a tool we can use to travel consciously through realities we already travel through unconsciously in our sleep every night. Its purpose serves simply to give you more awareness of how you can use and apply what you learn through your travels to your physical life.

So, you can anticipate encountering all these fascinating things during meditation. And of course, as you continue your practice more frequently, you will discover a great many other experiences that I have not had the time to discuss here.

Please know that as meditation becomes a big part of your daily life, it will give your spiritual journey a lot more power as well as enhance the quality of your life.

SCIENCE-BASED BENEFITS

Many scientific tests have been done on meditation and on people who meditate in general to find out how meditation affects the mind, the brain, our thoughts, and our overall health. The results of the experiments show that meditating is good for people and makes us happier.

I want to provide some scientific facts regarding meditation that show how it can benefit your life.

Science has shown that meditation can help reduce stress, which is good for your emotional health.

As it calms us down, it also increases our attention span. This makes us less likely to lose our memories as we get older, and it actually improves memory retention.

Meditation can help us get over our addictions, be more kind, and sleep better.

Next, meditation may help decrease blood pressure and assist people in controlling overall pain.

Lastly, meditation can be done anywhere at any time of the day. All you need is your breath, a comfortable spot, and the willingness to do so.

THE PERFECT POSTURE

Many people think that when practicing meditation, you need to have perfect posture. They think you need to be sitting in lotus pose, where both of your feet are right above your thighs, which makes it very difficult for those of us who are not flexible enough to do so.

When it comes to meditation, it is not necessary to have the most perfect posture in the world in order to fall into the proper state of meditation. Meditation posture strictly has to do with comfortability. As long as you are comfortable with the way that you are sitting or lying, to the point where you are capable of being in that position for an extended period of time, this is all that matters.

Of course, the spine does need to be as straight as possible without compromising comfortability. Your spine needs to be straight in order to allow a perfect flow of cosmic energy to channel through it, down your spinal cord, into your chakra system, and throughout your body. This is why keeping a straight spine is essential when meditating and making sure that we are one hundred percent comfortable.

We can sit or lie anywhere in the world that we feel comfortable—on a pillow, a chair, a bed, the floor, a rock; it really does not matter. Many people like to meditate while lying flat on their backs. This is not a position that I recommend for beginners because they tend to nod off while laying in this position.

Once you have been able to attain the meditative state of being quite a few times and have become accustomed to meditating in this way, perhaps you can try lying flat on your back. Your accumulated experience will most likely keep you from falling asleep when lying down.

THE FOGGING A MIRROR METHOD

About three or four years ago, I released a *Learn How to Meditate With CrewZ* course for anyone teaching people everything they needed to know about meditation. Many of you who bought this course have given me only positive feedback, and I love, appreciate, and am thankful for each and every one of you. I see how much it has helped you guys.

Helping people learn how to breathe properly through their diaphragm, along with the other beautiful spiritual practices that help guide people into further enlightenment, is something that I do because it brings me genuine happiness to know that I am doing *Spirit* work to benefit humanity.

So, again, thank you guys for purchasing this course. For any readers who are interested in checking it out, please visit www.meditatewithcrewz.thinkific.com. When you visit this link, you will be able to view and purchase this course.

In my course, I used a method called the "Fogging a Mirror Method." I have found it to be the most successful and effective way to teach a person how to properly breathe through their diaphragm.

Many people do not know this, but humans are born and designed to breathe through the diaphragm. As we grow up in a toxic world and environment, facing the stresses, anxieties, and fears of life, we begin to shift into survival-mode-breathing, losing touch with the natural way we are supposed to breathe.

The next time you are close to a sleeping baby, observe the baby's stomach. You will realize that the baby's stomach is going up and down and up and down while the baby is breathing and sleeping. This is because, as I mentioned, we are born naturally breathing through our diaphragms. It is part of human design.

Through the "Fogging a Mirror Method," you are enabled to reconnect with that way of breathing again so that you can breathe the way you were designed to breathe. You will take in more oxygen and attract more cosmic energy into your body.

How is the "Fogging a Mirror Method" done?

The answer is quite simple. Do you remember when you were a child? Many of us, as children, would always fog mirrors or windows, draw little heart shapes, our initials, our name, or other such scribblings of childhood. The point is, most of us are familiar with this.

Here is how it works. If you grab your hand and place your palm about six inches in front of your mouth, I want you to exhale into your palm, the same way you would exhale to fog a mirror, making the actual loud sound that fogging a mirror makes as well. Put your hand in front of your face and fog the mirror. Take a deep breath in and release it into your palms.

Notice how, when you exhale to fog a mirror, it sounds louder, deeper, thicker, stronger. When you exhale to fog a mirror, you are exhaling out of your diaphragm. Notice the difference in the sound and how loud it is.

Now, I want you to inhale back in the same way you exhaled to fog that mirror. When you do this, you will be breathing in through the diaphragm, and your mouth should still be open.

Do this a few times to become used to using your diaphragm with each inhalation and exhalation, as if fogging a mirror.

Once you have done this quite a few times with your mouth open, I want you to continue to fog the mirror, but this time, do it with your lips completely sealed, and then inhale back in the same way you exhaled to fog that mirror, keeping your lips completely sealed.

Instantly, you should notice a difference in your breathing. You will feel the pit of your stomach inflating instead of your chest. You will notice that you can actually take in a larger amount of oxygen.

If you do it long enough, deeply enough, and soothingly enough, you will realize how relaxed this type of breathing may cause you to feel. This is the natural way that you are supposed to be breathing 24/7.

You should now begin retraining your brain to breathe normally with your diaphragm. Keep this in mind and make the deliberate choice and effort to breathe via the diaphragm whenever you are not speaking, such as while you are walking, driving, showering, or going about your daily routine.

Never force yourself to inhale and exhale deeply through the diaphragm. Let it be a natural, rhythmic flow. Breathe through the diaphragm consciously, but at your own pace. The more that you do this, the more you will rewire your brain for this type of breathing. Hopefully, it will become second nature.

Diaphragmatic breathing helps us strengthen our lungs because the diaphragm acts as a lung muscle. By using and training the diaphragm in the right way, you can make your lungs stronger and be able to hold your breath for longer. You can also regulate your blood pressure with diaphragmatic breathing.

Learn to control your breathing, and you will learn to control your life. It is essential for expanding one's awareness and realizing one's hidden potential. The ability to do so is crucial for maintaining a healthy internal temperature. It is the secret to keeping your cool under pressure and keeping your mind and emotions in check.

Your breath is everything. Please make it a priority to master diaphragmatic breathing. You can do it.

Once you get to the point where you are comfortable with diaphragmatic breathing, there is a very powerful meditation I want you to try. It is called the "Ananda Mandala" meditation. The Ananda Mandala is an ancient meditation that the Indian seers passed down for thousands of years.

When we do the powerful Ananda Mandala meditation, we increase the strength of our diaphragms and fill our chakra system with energy through a series of fast inhalations and exhalations. The Ananda Mandala meditation will leave you feeling sensations and rushes of energy in your body that I am sure you have never felt before. It is life-changing—an energy booster.

If you do the Ananda Mandala meditation every day, you will start to develop some serious mental and psychic abilities. This is because the meditation really activates each of your chakras, which allows the totality of your consciousness to flow through you.

I would like to add that, because your brain is not currently wired to breathe in this way, you might feel lightheaded or dizzy when you first begin consciously practicing diaphragmatic breathing. This is perfectly normal, though, and it is okay to acknowledge that you are not used to this type of breathing. Feeling lightheaded or dizzy is actually a normal symptom when you first start getting back into breathing through the diaphragm.

As long as you stay consistent in the diaphragmatic breathing process, you will see rather quickly, within the first few days, how that light-headedness and dizziness will disappear and most likely not come back again.

As you strengthen your diaphragm, you also strengthen your lungs so that you can breathe this way permanently for the rest of your life.

Continue meditating, rising toward enlightenment, and penetrating through your reality. This beautiful meditation journey will only bring you closer to becoming the ultimate human.

Musical Vibes for this chapter
Search: **CrewZ - Spirit Ninja**
https://song.link/us/i/1472935649

The Maharishi Effect

THE MAHARISHI EFFECT is named after Maharishi Mahesh Yogi. He taught that if just one percent of the world's people practiced transcendental meditation at the same time, we could peacefully and naturally make this planet a better place to live. This is a concept that he first began speaking about in 1959.

According to the Maharishi principle, at least one percent of any population can affect and create positive change, whether it is a city, state, country, or the entire planet. However, there was an extended version with a new formula that was added to the Maharishi Effect, which states that only the square root of one percent of the population is actually enough to create and affect positive trends as well as neutralize any negative ones.

In 1974, there were eleven U.S. cities where the first experiments like this were conducted, in which participating groups reached one percent of the population of each city. Each group began to practice the transcendental meditation technique.

During the time that these groups were simultaneously meditating, crime rates in each city went down significantly. Researchers were shocked by this, so they decided to call it the "Maharishi Effect" in honor of the man who had predicted this would happen fifteen years earlier.

At the end of 1983, Maharishi got together seven thousand people, which at the time was about the square root of one percent of the world's population. He gathered all of these people to create what he called "A Taste of Utopia." The goal of this event was to have all seven thousand people do transcendental meditation at the same time to see what kind of effect it would have on the world.

According to a content analyst for the New York Times and the London Times, the meditation of these seven thousand people caused international conflicts to decrease by more than thirty percent. Even international terrorism decreased by a whopping seventy-two percent. They also saw an increase in economic confidence.

The great thing about these experiments is that since they worked, more than fifty studies on the Maharishi Effect have been done. These studies have indicated the power of meditation to transform global tendencies. It demonstrated that people are capable of moving mountains if we just work together and choose to breathe deeply through our diaphragms and elevate the frequencies of our being.

We can accomplish such things all while holding the intention of healing the world, reducing crime, and creating more peace, harmony, and positivity around the world. Human beings are magnificent creatures, and when we unite together, we are capable of things beyond our wildest dreams.

Another group of four thousand people gathered in Washington, D.C., from June 7th to July 30th, 1993. A government think-tank project was established to observe the experiment. The National Demonstration Project was organized to cut down on violent crime and improve government work. They were a twenty-seven-member independent project review board composed of sociologists and criminologists. Civic leaders, police officers, and people from the government of the District of Columbia were all there to monitor the experiment.

It was noted that many violent crimes, such as rape, assaults, and homicides, would continue to decrease as the meditation group got larger and more people began to join in. The maximum decrease in this experiment was a little more than twenty-three percent when the meditation group was at its largest.

It is due to studies like these that my mind cannot help but love the practice of meditation. I love what it can turn us into, what it can give us access to, and what it can help us understand on our journey to becoming the ultimate human.

The fact that meditation alone can help heal the world and lower the crime rate is just amazing. People simply need to create massive meditation parties. It is my belief that we can turn around so much of the negativity that we see in this world today. Because our minds are all connected via the collective planetary consciousness grid of humanity, it is only a matter of time before a small group of people produces a completely new reality for the rest of the billions who have no idea what is happening.

I wanted to make sure that I included a reference to the Maharishi Effect in your quest to become the ultimate human. These are things we need to know about. Although so many people do know about these things, there is still a vast majority of us who have no idea what meditation is capable of creating in this world.

We can all create and achieve the kind of beauty, harmony, and positivity that we all want to see every day. All we need to do is teach more people what is possible with just their breath.

This is why I have become and will always be a powerful advocate for meditation.

I have experienced firsthand what meditation was able to do for me and how it has increased my intelligence. I have seen what it has done to loved ones. I am aware of others who also meditate and how much it has affected and uplifted them. I am sure that if everyone else did the same thing, we could make the world the most peaceful place in human history.

Mass education is needed, and the best way to do this is by educating one soul at a time, then through group settings, mass speeches, and worldwide meditation parties.

I hope you will join me in developing events like this, where we can come together safely and quietly to heal the earth. When this day happens, it will bring such joy to my heart to witness a large number of people gathered together in person to meditate for the sake of world peace.

We are powerful. We can do it. I believe in all of us. I just need you to believe in us too.

Musical Vibes for this chapter
Search: **CrewZ - Infinite Waters**
https://song.link/us/i/1465340414

Humanity

THERE IS GOING to come a point where you have to gain some humanity during this journey of yours toward becoming the ultimate human. I know there are a lot of you out there who do not like people, who do not like to deal with people, who are not comfortable being around other people. I understand that your life experiences from the past are what led you to be this way.

I want you to understand that there is nothing wrong with this.

Do not feel bad.

This is who you are right now.

If you are currently not someone who deals very well with people or who does not trust people based on your past experiences, this is who you are. Everything takes time. One day, everyone will be exactly where they need to be. That is something you must trust. You must always trust the process.

However, if this beautiful spiritual journey is going to

teach us one thing, it is that we are an integrated aspect of everyone else. Everyone is connected to everyone, regardless of what human life entails, how people look, or where they come from. Everybody is connected to everybody.

This is a science that cannot be debated. It is a fact in terms of consciousness.

We are all connected to each other. We are all connected to our planet. We are all connected to animals. We are all connected to nature and the weather. We are connected to everything. The sooner you realize and accept this, the sooner you will stop seeing a disconnect between you and your reality.

If you are going to awaken and embark on the path of becoming the ultimate human, you are going to have to realize that that also entails you having to deal with people, building community, working together, picking each other's brains, and many collaborations.

People need to regain a sense of humanity. If we want to work toward enlightenment and believe that we can reach fourth density and beyond, we need to come together and work as one. Unity is what humanity strives for.

WHEN WE COME TOGETHER and stand united, we are a force that is untouchable and impenetrable. Collectively, we are capable of creating anything we set our minds to. Because of this, it is more important than ever for humanity to choose love as we stand at the crossroads of our spiritual development.

We must choose compassion and empathy for one another, promising to help and support one another when we need it. We must choose to understand that everyone is in their own process, and each of us will get where we need to go in our own time.

Stop judging others. We must let go of outdated preconceptions about how people should be or what is right or wrong, realizing that everyone has their own perspective of right and wrong, good and bad.

Nobody is going to ever be exactly how you want them to be. That is okay. You need to be okay with that.

I cannot stress enough how important it is for you to have some sense of humanitarianism. You need to be able to look at this earth and want it to heal. You need to be able to look at human beings that you do not know—complete strangers—and want the best for them. You want them to succeed, to heal and find love, and to become the best version of themselves possible. Why? Because remember, you are an aspect of all that is, and humanity is a reflection of you.

If you want to heal yourself, you must first choose to love yourself.

When you finally get to that point where you have healed yourself, you will want to assist others to accomplish the same. Everyone who is reading this will experience it in their own special way.

Each of you brings something special to the earth. All of you will eventually realize how much you can contribute, how talented you are, and how much you can do that you may not even be aware of yet. However, you all possess it, and you are all traveling in search of the same goal. That is the thing that is going to bring you fulfillment. It will bring you internal happiness. That long sigh of relief that you are all waiting for is attainable. In your own way, it is attainable.

Humanity is at a point where it now needs to make a

decision for itself on a collective mass scale. We have to decide whether we want to keep learning the same lessons of third density—of good and evil, of suffering and pleasure.

Do you still want to experience this?

Or is your soul ready for the next phase in soul evolution? Are you ready to enter the fourth density? Are you ready to be a more harmonic and cohesive human being? To bring about this change, you guys need to choose this. It is more important now than ever. The window of opportunity is closing, so now is the time to step fully into our power, fully cultivate ourselves, choose to heal, choose to stay in the frequency of unconditional love and intelligence, and choose to have a sense of humanity.

We need to do things for this planet. Anything that we can do to come together, we need to do now more than ever.

Our current civilization on earth today is the fifth civilization.

I believe there have been four civilizations prior to the one that exists on earth today. Some historians speculate that the great flood, which occurred about 13,000 years ago and was concomitant with the fall of Atlantis, was the end of the fourth civilization. It looks like the four civilizations that came before us perished by each of the elements. The last one being by the element of water.

We are the fifth civilization, which represents the fifth element. The fifth element is *Spirit* and we are the civilization that is destined to intertwine with it. It is now our choice. Are we going to choose to reintegrate our *Spirit* with the elemental *Spirit* and graduate to the next level? Or will we remain in the third density? Many individuals have and will continue to shift their consciousnesses to fourth Density. The goal, however, is for the masses to do it.

Presently, the earth has chosen to ascend. It is up to the people who live on it to decide whether to ascend with the earth or stay in the dualistic universe. The choice is yours. We are living in what is referred to as the "Splitting of Worlds," and we are seeing it manifest right before our very eyes.

We see it happening in our world today, in 2023. We can clearly see the divide in humanity. There is a clear distinction between those who choose to live more consciously and those who choose to live in fear. For the super conscious folks, you can clearly see the people who resonate more with the fourth density frequencies, and those souls who are not ready, who will continue the cycle of reincarnation until they are ready. It is no secret now. The powers that be no longer care to hide anything from you. They are letting you know what is up at this point.

Either you are going to give in to this low frequency and keep talking nonsense, or you are going to give yourself a higher purpose.

You are going to choose love and reach for the highest frequency of intelligence. You are going to choose to unify and come together to create communities and sacred spaces where everyone can elevate such frequencies collectively. This is what's going to make a change in this world.

Every single artist out there has an audience waiting to receive their gift. Every single one of you has a gift to contribute to humanity's awakening. I believe it is true for every single one of you. I do not care how worthless you think you are or how untalented you think you are. It does not matter.

Every single person alive today has an incredible gift to contribute to humanity's awakening into the Fourth density and beyond. And now, more than ever, is the time for you to reach the point where you can manifest this for yourself, where you can make a difference on this planet.

I have given you a lot of information in this book that you can look into further, make your own, act on, and bring into your life. This is the kind of life you deserve to live: a spiritually fulfilled life, a life full of inner happiness, and a life in which you are your godlike self.

Indeed, you are an aspect of God. You have simply forgotten this.

Becoming the ultimate human means realizing that you are an aspect of God. It means embarking on the path of self-realization and staying true to your practice. When you realize this truth and accept it for what it is, it will be much easier for you to align yourself with your true, authentic self.

We all have that self-image of ourselves that we have created for ourselves. However, there is a difference between the self we have created for ourselves and our true authentic self. Our true authentic self is who we are when no one is looking, when we are by ourselves, talking to ourselves in the mirror, or perhaps, acting on behaviors that we would never ever show anyone outside of ourselves.

All of us struggle with the duality of the self.

We create a self shown only to society, and on the other hand, there is the self we cradle as our authentic self.

It is now time to get real with yourself and to show more of your true authentic self, the person you really are when no one is looking. You want to reveal the person who becomes wiser through time and becomes more in tune with themselves vibrationally. Do this so that you can continue to create a life that fits more and more with who you think you are.

You will begin to see many new experiences set in motion that will bring you closer to your life's purpose as you practice consistency and apply this information to your current lifestyle.

In terms of why your soul chose to be here at this time in the first place, you will get closer and closer to accomplishing your soul's purpose.

The more you choose to act upon these things and stay consistent in these spiritual practices, the more your heart will grow to a size that you could never have imagined before. This will lead you to feel this internal oneness with all things, with all life forms, with all humans. Naturally, you will gain this compassion, this humanitarianism, that is required.

As you ascend to higher and higher states of consciousness, you will naturally be in tune with all beings, and you will love to talk to people again. You will no longer fear communication, run away from communication, or feel some kind of dreadful energy towards communication. You will now see how simple it is to communicate with other aspects of yourself. We are all aspects of one another.

I have to continuously repeat this because it is something you have to see over and over again, bombarding your subconscious mind until you finally realize that this is what it is. This realization alone is what is going to help humanity achieve peace — the realization that we are all one. The realization that when we hurt another, we are hurting ourselves. When we assist another, we are assisting ourselves. We need to think in this way, collectively.

When one of us is rich, we are all rich. If one of us is down, we are all down. We need to think like this. This is what will bring humanity back as a unified force.

When looking at humans, you must be able to see beyond the human form. Peer directly into the eyes and see the soul that is animating that human form. You must see beyond a person's gender, identity, skin color, speech, and expression when engaging with them. It is important to see the level of awareness at which the soul operates.

By being consciously able to see their level of awareness, you will be able to know how to deal with that being. You will know how to reflect the frequency required for them to understand you. You will know how to persuade all types of people.

I am giving you my personal secret sauce on how I am able to communicate with any human being, regardless of the walk of life they come from or what experiences they have been through. At this point in my life, I can reflect any frequency back to any person. I have had enough human interaction to be able to do this.

Because I am in tune with everyone, I understand this. I love everyone unconditionally in secret, regardless of how dysfunctional they may act in front of me. I am aware of the factors that make such behavior possible for them, and I am deciding to let myself accept what is happening when they are in this low-frequency state. I too make mistakes and sometimes get caught up in ego. I am not perfect and this path is a non-stop work in progress. Regardless of how much I may allow myself to get consumed by this illusion of separation momentarily, I am always able to pull myself out of it and return to love.

When you get to this level of understanding and also see the world in this way, you will naturally feel a loving sensation toward everyone. You will want everyone to win, to make it, and to be successful. You will want to support all of them and make it happen, regardless of who they are. Because now you see that you are everyone; everyone is you. Let us all be there for each other the way we need to be.

There are many different stages that civilizations must go through as they choose to go up the evolutionary ladder. They progress from being simple creatures unable to leave their home planet to beings capable of traveling through space and communicating with other galactic societies that have attained the same or a higher level of consciousness. This is already happening.

These beings are waiting for us and our planet to get to that point. We need to grow spiritually as a whole before we can handle space travel. In 2023, we are still not there.

But I do see the acceleration of consciousness that has been happening. I do believe that humanity is on a path towards that. How fast this will happen for us collectively depends on us. What do we choose to do from here? How do we choose to go about what is going on in the world today? How do we choose to combat this? Are we going to fight fire with fire? Or are we going to choose to vibrate higher? That is the question here for all of us to ponder. We need to choose to go higher. It is time. Earth has suffered enough.

WE NO LONGER WANT TO BE IN a world full of divisiveness, separation, war, hatred, and a lack of effective communication. We have been in spiritual warfare on this planet for a very long time, and I believe this war will show us all, once and for all, that it is time for people to take a stand against those who oppress us and enslave us, and to remind them that we call the shots here. We no longer need them to lead us. They work for humanity.

At this point in history, when humanity has been going through a long period of spiritual evolution, the earth needs people to wake up, unite, build communities around the world, and practice more stillness, unconditional love, and compassion than ever before.

I will always be a vessel for this truth and this message because it is the highest frequency that can exist, and the earth deserves to resonate and vibrate at the highest frequency so that she can show us her true beauty and nature can work with us instead of against us. We can be connected with nature again, with animals again, with all of humanity, the stars, and beyond.

THE KARDASHEV SCALE

Yet, humanity is not even considered a true civilization yet. Let me explain what I mean by that. In 1964, there was a Russian astrophysicist by the name of Nikolai Kardashev. Experts say that as a civilization gets more advanced and bigger, its energy needs will also grow quickly. This is because the population is always growing and the machines that people keep making and inventing need more and more energy.

The Kardashev scale was developed as a way of measuring a civilization's technological advancement. This is done based upon how much usable energy a civilization has at its disposal. In 1964, when Nikolai Kardashev invented the Kardashev scale, he was looking for signs of extraterrestrial life within cosmic signals.

The Kardashev scale was divided into three base civilization classes, each with an energy disposal level.

- Type I energy level 10 to the 16th watt
- Type II energy level 10 to the 26th watt
- Type III energy level 10 to the 36th watt

Other astronomers have added Type IV and Type V civilizations to the scale over time.

What I find extremely hard to believe, but at the same time, I am not surprised, is that our current civilization on earth today is not even on the Kardashev scale yet. We are technically considered a Type 0 civilization. For our planet to become a Type I civilization, we still have to go through our natural and spiritual evolution processes. This is not an easy task, and it could take thousands of years for a race or civilization to achieve Type I status.

We will still be classified as a Type 0 civilization because we get our energy from dead plants, animals, fossil fuels, etc. This is a very primitive way for a civilization to sustain itself via energy. If we are ever going to evolve and become a Type One civilization, there is definitely some leveling up that must occur.

First, we need to figure out how a Type I civilization gets enough energy to keep going. A species that reaches Type I is able to harness all of the energy that is available to them from their planet. They collect and store this energy to meet the growing energy needs of people.

If we were able to use all of the earth's energy, we would

also have full control over all of nature's forces. This means that humans could control the weather, earthquakes, tsunamis, volcanoes, and even the earth's gravitational pull. This will lead humans to stop the extraction of minerals from the earth's interior. We will become fully eco-friendly because of our ability to generate electricity from almost everything on this planet.

Once we reach a Type II civilization, we will be able to control the energy of the sun and the rest of the solar system.

To give us a visual understanding of what that would look like, it is appropriate that I mention the American physicist by the name of Freeman Dyson, who came up with a hypothetical sphere that is now named after him. The Dyson Sphere is a huge sphere that is in the form of a shell and is so huge that it has the ability to engulf the entire sun. Its main purpose is to extract energy from a central star.

This development would mean that a Type II civilization is incapable of being wiped out. They have risen above suffering, and they cannot die out or destroy themselves because they are able to control huge amounts of energy. Any astronomical threat to destroy Earth would be easy for a Type II civilization.

At the Type II level, civilization will be able to travel through space. They will be able to go to nearby planets and stars, where they can meet other galactic societies that have already reached this level of development.

A Type I civilization is a group of people who are able to use all the energy on their home planet. A Type II civilization is a group of people who are able to use all of the energy from a star.

Let us move on to a Type III civilization.

When a civilization reaches this level of energetic

mastery, that species will be capable of harnessing the energy of an entire galaxy. With Dyson spheres, every planet and star in the Milky Way galaxy would be contained and their energy harnessed. One can only imagine the types of abilities and capabilities a civilization would have if it were able to sustain the energy of an entire galaxy.

At this point, Nikolai Kardashev felt that it would be impossible for a civilization to go beyond this. Therefore, he left it at three different types of civilizations within the scale.

However, as I mentioned before, there are other astrophysicists who ended up adding on to the Kardashev scale, types IV and V. We will include this as well, so you guys have an understanding of what else may be possible for a civilization that is capable of going beyond a Type III civilization. What does this even look like?

If Type I is harnessing the energy of a planet, Type II is harnessing the energy of a star, and Type III is harnessing the energy of a galaxy, then it only makes sense that Type IV would mean that a civilization is capable of harnessing the energy of multiple galaxies at the same time, which would also give them the ability to travel anywhere throughout any region of our universe.

If you go one step further to Type V, you could say it is a civilization that can control or use the energy of the entire universe in which they live. At this point, you could say that this level of civilization is kind of like playing God because they have the capability of doing as they please and going wherever they please within their universe.

I have also read some information from others who have included a Type VI on the scale, which would be super far-fetched for the average human to try and fathom. A Type VI is pretty much the same as saying that you have become god and can create and destroy multiple universes at will and instantly.

So, what have we learned in this chapter? We have learned that humanity is connected at the subatomic and core levels. All of us are aspects of each other as *Spirit*. All of us are connected to each other, our planet, nature, animals, stars, galaxies, the entire universe, and creation itself.

We all affect one another through cause and effect and our intentions.

We also learned that we must gain a sense of humanity and humanitarianism if we are to step into and embody becoming the ultimate human. You must have compassion in your heart and unconditional love for all people. You must know in your mind that love and compassion are the only ways we can come together, heal the planet, and move on to the next level of our evolution.

We learned about the Kardashev Scale and how it may be used to categorize civilizations based on their energy output.

Hopefully, this eye-opening chapter gave you more insight as to how beautiful, amazing, and powerful humanity is, as well as the potential we have ahead of us and how great life will become after we are gone, if and only if humanity decides to go down this path towards fourth density.

Love one another, empower one another, inspire one another, be there, and support one another, because we are all we have. Humanity has to ascend to the next level spiritually, and we are not spiritually mature enough to do it yet.

We will get there by exposing our minds to these truths, to this awareness, and by studying the science of *Spirit*. This is how we will attain the global peace for which we innately yearn.

Musical Vibes for this chapter
Search: **CrewZ - Have You Ever**
https://song.link/us/i/1465340400

The Breath

OUR BREATH IS PERHAPS the most valuable thing in all of human existence. This is so because, without your breath, there is no life, only death to meet. People need to breathe in order to exist within this realm of physicality. The breath is what attaches our consciousness to the body.

When humans become old, it becomes more difficult for consciousness or to keep that attachment to the body as much as it used to during its younger years. Most humans don't take good care of their health as they age and end up on all sorts of prescriptions and medications just to get by without some degree of pain or discomfort. This is an indication that the energy body is heavily depleted and solely now relying on external substances to function properly or to even function at all.

The older a person becomes, the more stiff their bodies get from the many years of not maintaining some flexibility in the body. This causes less cosmic energy to flow through the body's system. Due to so many years of not eating well, inactivity in exercise, overthinking, stress and anxiety, negative self-talk, or just being in a low-frequency state of being in general, the body will begin to diminish and decay.

Over time, a person will find themselves breathing less and less, taking shorter, quicker breaths—the ultimate survival mode for breathing. It is easy to see just how valuable the breath is to human existence. Literally, mastering one's breath gives access to all kinds of superhuman skills and abilities, not to mention, our bodies operating at full capacity of energy. This is why learning how to breathe with the diaphragm is so important for anyone who wants to operate at their best.

Now, let us think about this pragmatically. Once you are able to train your mind to breathe through the diaphragm as often as you consciously can, you will realize over time that this new strength in your lungs will let you consciously control your breath.

What I mean by this is that you will be capable of controlling how slowly and how fast you inhale and exhale. Tortoises are known to be able to live for up to one hundred plus years. And through science, we have learned that the tortoise can take only four breaths per minute. There are also many other animals that breathe slower than humans and live long as well. This shows that the slower we breathe, the longer we could possibly live.

Therefore, if you find yourself stuck breathing in survival mode, taking quick, short breaths, you will realize that continuing breathing this way will bring you closer and closer to death.

Do your best to practice to breathing smoothly through very long, deep inhalations and deep exhalations through the diaphragm. Do this consciously day in and day out, either while you are driving, showering, or doing any activity that doesn't require you to speak. Always consciously breathe through the diaphragm and fill up with as much oxygen as you can each time.

What this will do for you over time is give you the ability to control your breath. This will lead you to learn how to control your emotional state, how to consciously create the thoughts you prefer to have, as well as how to expand your ability to comprehend. Just as your lungs are expanding, so is your consciousness.

Always make it a priority to breathe through your diaphragm, and your overall human experience will get better over time. I have read a lot of things about people with superhuman abilities. Oftentimes, all of these people have one thing in common: their breathing.

Many of these people have learned through training with a spiritual guru or master or by meditating on their own that learning how to do certain breathing techniques and combining them with the meditative practice of meditation is what allows them to do these things. Humans can even regulate their own body temperatures through their breath alone. But, of course, it takes guidance and consistency, as well as learning how to control the breath via the diaphragm.

There are people today who can be in a very cold environment, like in the snow, and yet still be able to sit there and breathe without being affected by the cold. These people have learned how to control the temperature of their bodies simply through their breath.

For a lot of us, we take breathing for granted. Because breathing is not something we consciously do, since our body is breathing for us on autopilot, we tend not to think much about the breath. We do not see how important and vital our breath is to our entire life. And so, once we finally make the conscious decision and choice to say, "You know what, let me observe this beautiful force of intelligence that is giving me life right now." Only then will we better understand its importance. What is the mystery behind our breath? What is the science behind this? Start asking yourself these questions and become intrigued by your breath.

Right now, as you are hearing or reading these words, take notice of your breath. Are you even breathing? Or are you holding your breath right now? Are you taking deep, deep inhalations in slow breaths, or are you breathing quickly in survival mode?

Take really good notice of what your breath is doing right now.

Then, as you hear or read these words, right now, at this moment, take a deep diaphragmatic breath through the pit of your stomach and inhale until you can no longer inhale. Once you have done that, hold your breath for about three to five seconds, and simply observe the sensations in your body with your eyes closed.

After three to five seconds, release and exhale all of that air out of your diaphragm until you can no longer exhale.

Once you do this, I want you to inhale back in through the diaphragm, but this time, do it as slowly as you possibly can. Once you're done, release your breath like normal and then repeat the process until you no longer want to.

Keep on doing this continuously, train your brain, rewire your brain for this process.

What you are doing right now is strengthening your diaphragm by learning to control your breathing. This is why I asked you to breathe as slowly as you can, and why I asked you to inhale and exhale until there is nothing left to inhale or exhale.

What I want you to do is become a master at breathing through your diaphragm because there are so many benefits that will come to your life once you learn how to properly breathe and get out of survival mode breathing.

There is a person whose story I would like to share. Perhaps many of you have heard of him, but if not, I believe now is a good time to mention him. In 1988, two English brothers made a documentary, which included him, called "Ring of Fire: An Indonesian Odyssey." They had heard stories about a unique acupuncturist named John Chang, (who people also called "Dynamo Jack").

John Chang is a unique human being who has unusual spiritual abilities. He is a man who had been practicing meditation every day for eighteen years at the time of the documentary's recording. John was proficient in the art of Mo Pai Nei Kung. He was trained by his master and eventually he was able to build up high levels of energy in his body. John Chang was capable of transferring this energy within him through his hands and into the needles in his patients' bodies, thus healing their illnesses and pains.

The two English brothers had traveled to meet him in hopes that he could heal one of the brothers' eye infections. Using acupuncture, Chang was able to manifest large amounts of energy, effectively curing the infections. His approach seemed almost miraculous and inspired the brothers to produce more footage of him doing other unique things with his abilities.

You can watch this story on Youtube.com by searching for the name John Chang, where you will find some clips taken from that documentary. When they asked him, "How is it that you are capable of transferring this energy? Is it because you were born with a special gift? What is it that gives you this ability?" John Chang replied, "Meditation every day."

John shared he had been meditating every day for eighteen years and that the practice of meditation gave him the ability to control his two lower chakra centers. He said that he could get the negative energy and the positive energy from the lower chakras and bring them together in balance and harmony. When he did this, it created and generated a form of electricity in his body at will.

He could then direct that energy through his hands into the needle and into the bodies of his clients, whom he was treating.

John Chang goes on to say that this energy, or this ability that he has, can heal, but it can also be very dangerous. It can also kill people if you do not know how to control your emotional state or your thoughts. "Great power comes with great responsibility." And that statement is very appropriate here.

When you start meditating and make it a regular part of your life, you will find that it makes you more loving, compassionate, empathetic, and understanding toward people, animals, and life in general. So, in my opinion, if you meditate for many years and then acquire a skill like John Chang's, it is hard to imagine that you will use that skill to hurt or take advantage of other people.

There is just no reason for it.

At this point, you have reached such a high degree of awareness within yourself that once you gain this skill, like John Chang's, you will have no such purpose; it will not cross your mind to commit such an act. All of this energy you have cultivated will only raise the frequency of your intelligence and increase your connection to nature and the divine spirit within you. You will naturally, because of your vibration, want to do nothing but good things and heal as many people and things on this planet as possible.

This is why mastering the breath is so essential. We must learn how to control our thoughts and our emotional state consciously. If we can learn to control our breathing, we can learn to control our emotions and intentionally create the thoughts we want. This is how we will create healing in our mental health; healing in our susceptibility to becoming lost in the illusion of separation; and healing of racism, which is based on the illusion of separation. Believing that we are all different and separate from each other is what can cause something as ridiculous as racism.

I hope you guys can see now why the breath is such an important topic of conversation to have when dealing with spiritual conversations, meditations, and embarking on the path of becoming the ultimate human.

To be the ultimate human, you have to be able to do everything that it means to be human. Almost all of us on planet Earth right now are not even operating at our full human potential yet. Yes, of course, we are within these human bodies. We live and experience through these human bodies, but none of us is really living up to our full, one-hundred percent true, human potential.

I know from my many years of being on the spiritual journey that by mastering our breathing, it may aid and assist us greatly in being able to heal many sicknesses, pains, low-frequency perspectives, and to bring a sense of belonging to fill that void where you still feel like something is missing in your life.

Meditation, persistent practices, mastering diaphragmatic breathing, spending more time in nature, exhibiting more empathy and compassion towards people, and displaying more empathy and compassion towards animals are all ways to bring a sense of inner contentment and fulfillment into your human life experience. These are the things that will bring you the happiness that you are seeking and the fulfillment that you wish to experience in your life. A combination of all of these things is needed for us to be capable of operating at our full potential as human beings.

I do not want to make it seem as though I am telling you that if you simply master your breath, all your problems are going to go away and you are going to become a fully self-actualized and healed human. Obviously, there is a lot more that goes into this if you want to heal and become the ultimate human. But what I am saying is that if you make it your goal and top priority to master diaphragmatic breathing and master your consistency in meditating as much as you can, as often as you can, you will conceive and create a whole new level of experience in your life.

By mastering the breath, you are raising the frequency of your own consciousness. When you raise the frequency of your intelligence, you can tap into new ways to solve problems and look at things that you could not think of before because you did not have the knowledge or the breath power that is needed for a human to maintain such high frequencies of understanding.

And so, yes, I am telling you that breathing is a very important thing to master.

But I do not want you to get it twisted and think that, by my telling you these things, all you have to do is master breathing, take no action on other necessities, and all of your problems will be solved. Of course, this is not the case.

Breathing is a huge aspect of becoming an ultimate human, of course, but it is not everything. A healthy diet, exercise, spiritual practices, practicing compassion, diaphragm work, and energy work are also very important to your success.

Humanity needs to get back in touch with a lot of different things in order to fully realize its true potential, the God-like powers that lie dormant in all of us.

I hope I have inspired you in some way to practice more and more conscious *breathing through the diaphragm* and to take these things seriously. I mean, hey, you are here reading a book called *Becoming the Ultimate Human*. Obviously, there is something within you that is interested in this topic.

I hope that by now you have a good idea of what kind of commitment it takes to become the ultimate human.

SEXUAL ENERGY

When we talk about the breath and how to control it, we must also bring up the subject of sexual energy. We live on a planet where most people use and abuse their sexual energy in detrimental ways.

What I mean by this is that we are all programmed to seek sex rather than to understand the power behind what we can do with our sexual energy.

Subliminal messages from the media have made us all want sex all the time. This is because we all grew up in a toxic environment full of lies and manipulation by the media and global organizations that want to control and enslave us.

None of us in America, through our educational system, has been properly informed about what sexual energy actually is and why and how it is extremely important to learn how to utilize it in the proper way. Nor have we been correctly educated on the *essential power* behind sexual energy.

Most of us seek to have sex simply to experience an orgasm. We all seek to have that peak orgasmic experience because we all yearn for such a high-frequency sensation. When our bodies reach a point of climax and orgasm, what we are experiencing at that moment is what it feels like, temporarily, for our consciousness to experience operating at such a high-frequency.

When you learn to consciously phase into a higher-dimensional reality, you will realize that the feelings you have are as orgasmic as those that happen during sex, if not more so.

Now that we are on this topic, it is important to understand the connection between the breath and sexual energy. Through the breath, we are capable of controlling not only our sexual urges but also the sexual energy that travels up our spine.

Now, what do I mean by this? Many times, when we feel the sensation, which some call "horny," what is happening, energetically speaking, is that our sacral chakras, which are located two to three inches below our belly button, begin to get activated. This is the body's vortex center, where our emotional and sexual energies live.

Once it is activated and fully spinning, you will feel the sensation of what some call horniness. Many of us do not know how to control this urge or how to consciously manipulate the energy that we feel and bring it up the spine.

"Why the spine?" you may ask.

Remember that your energy centers (chakras) are located from the base of the spine to the top of the head. When you consciously breathe in this sexual sensation and energy up the spine, you're directing an energy so powerful and capable of creating life itself, into the brain that then gets distributed throughout your body and into your other organs. This not only causes full-body orgasms, which last longer than a regular orgasm, but it also revitalizes the energy body and enhances your bodily functions over time. This is also very true when it comes to actually performing sexual acts or having sex. Men are actually capable of having multiple orgasms just like women can via this practice, and all without ejaculating!

During the moment of orgasm, if you can control the sensation via your breathing during sex and consciously bring that energy up the spine with your breath and visualization, you will learn to bring that sexual energy up into the brain, into your head point of consciousness.

Sexual energy is utilized in our manifestations.

When sexual energy is so powerful that it can create a whole life, learning how to cultivate it and direct it toward something meaningful, like something you want to create for yourself or into the organs of the body, makes your intention to create it bigger and stronger.

So, we are actually supposed to be utilizing our sexual energies towards our manifestations and creating optimal health and energy in the body. But instead, we have been programmed to just look for sex and keep letting this very powerful and important life force energy out.

When a man and a woman engage in sexual intercourse, if both parties are spiritually conscious and aware of their sexual energies and what they must do with them, the man will bring the energy up the spine through his breath, while the woman will bring the energy down the spine through her breath. What they are creating is called "toroidal field energy," which flows in and out of itself indefinitely.

This makes the sexual act a conscious exchange of energy between the two people involved. This is why it is very important that you choose wisely with whom you choose to exchange your sexual energies. You are taking in the entire consciousness of every single being that you have sex with, as well as everyone they've ever had sex with. For those of us with an extreme amount of sexual partner experiences, detoxing and cleansing of the auric field is required and highly suggested. Breath & energy work, chakra activation, plant-based dieting, and meditation are the best practices I have personally found to help cleanse and detox the auric field.

Once you both reach this point of orgasm and release and exchange sexual energies with each other, their consciousness literally becomes a part of your consciousness field and you'll take on all their energetic baggage.

Those of us who choose to have so many different sexual partners end up with what is known as a "mix of emotional energies." We are not capable of understanding why we have such a mixture of energies and emotional states and why we cannot control ourselves.

Those of us who have become sex addicts become mentally or emotionally unstable over time. This is because there have been so many exchanges of sexual energies with so many people. When you have a one-night stand, you do not know the frequency or the level of awareness at which that person is operating. And since you do not know this, for all you know, you could be having sex with someone who has murdered someone in the past, someone who is completely divisive, mentally speaking, or someone who has very low self-esteem or a very low frequency or quality of perception in themselves. And so, without realizing it, you are taking on their energy; you are making it your own.

It does not matter how physically attractive they may be. This is why you need to be very careful and very picky about who you choose to exchange your sexual energy with. Our breath is so powerful that we can use the same energy that makes a human life happen to bring about the life we want to live.

And just so that there is no confusion, I want to make it clear that when it comes to gay or bisexual couples, this information also pertains to them as well. We all have both masculine and feminine energies inside of us, no matter what our sexual orientation is or what gender we identify as.

If you are gay or bisexual, then know that this can also be done during your sexual engagement as well. During the sexual act, those of you who are mostly masculine dominant will focus on bringing the energy up the spine, while those of you who are more in tune with your feminine energies will focus on bringing the energy down the spine.

No matter what, we are all sexual beings. It is part of our nature, and we need to embrace this aspect of ourselves. However, we need to do it in an intelligent and healthy way. Society has taught people to show their sexual energy in a way that is too strong and hurtful.

Please, realize that it is perfectly okay to engage in sexual activity. But now that you have a better understanding of sexual energy, you must have a new perspective when engaging in sex. You must take notice of your breath, becoming more conscious and aware of it during sexual intercourse. Practice moving the energy up and down the spine while you are sexually active until your brain is rewired to do this.

You will notice that not only will your sexual experience improve, but you will also be able to use this powerful energy to create what you want in your life. So, happy breathing to you all. May you continue to elevate your human life experience through your breath. And may you all fully realize and embody your human potential.

Musical Vibes for this chapter
Search: **CrewZ - Cosmic Waves**
https://song.link/us/i/1465340406

The Ultimate Path

BRAHMA MEANS "The Ultimate of the Divine." Charya translates as "The Path." It is clear that a Brahmacharya is a person who is on the way to becoming the ultimate divine. And in so doing, one is also on the path to becoming the ultimate human.

All of you reading this right now, myself included, are working towards Brahmacharya. We are all now on the path to becoming the ultimate human and the ultimate divine.

We are embodying this frequency of the ultimate path back to the divine so that we can live it, feel it, and share it with the world.

Human beings are designed to emulate those of a higher frequency. When we are around someone who has honed their energies enough to raise their frequencies to the point where they can express such pure intelligence, it is only natural that their presence raises the frequency of our auras. This makes us feel attracted to them and want to be around them all the time. We always feel good in their presence because they uplift us.

Everyone who reads this should try to reach this level of being so that we can continue, individually and as a group, to uplift and inspire as many people and groups as we can on our way to the ultimate divine.

Everything you will read from now on is coming straight from my heart chakra. There is no research involved. I just want to end this book with words of wisdom that come from my heart space. I want to be as transparent as possible with you all.

This is the very first book I have ever written in my entire life. I never thought that I would, at some point in this incarnation, become the author of a book. I always thought writing a book would be something of an annoyance and would take years to do.

But here I am, at the age of thirty-three cycles around the sun, finishing a book called *Becoming the Ultimate Human* in the hopes that it will inspire millions—even billions—of people to follow the ultimate path back to the Divine.

All I want for this world is for it to heal and ascend to its next level of existence: fourth density. I am realizing now more than ever that the purpose of my being on this planet during these times, is simply to uplift, educate, inspire, heal, and empower people.

This is my true calling. And because this is my passion, I can use the skills and talents I have gained in my many lives before this one to channel this energy.

Through my hands, mind, and mouth, art, music, words, and expression, whether verbal or written, I bring my divine connection to the earth. I do everything that I can and channel this beautiful divine energy in any way that I can, in hopes of inspiring and uplifting humanity to claim their full potential.

I love this world. I love all its people. I love humanity because I know its true potential.

I know our worth. I know our birthright as humans on this planet is to be free and godlike. To restore kindness, generosity, tolerance, and empathy, we must establish the frequency of unconditional love, which is also the frequency of supreme intellect.

We must reach an in-depth mutual understanding of one another. There has to be a return to formalized training in interpersonal education and communication. Getting back to being telepathic will require us to hone in our mental and psychic abilities.

Through telepathy, we will eradicate miscommunication. There is no miscommunication when it comes to telepathy. It is instantaneous communication.

We are designed to communicate with each other through telepathy. Telepathy lets us understand each other without having to speak out loud. It does this by using sounds, tastes, smells, touches, and everything else we can feel or sense. Because of this, the person you are sharing your knowledge and experiences with may visualize, smell, taste, and hear everything you did while going through the experience you were describing to them. Therefore, there is no room for miscommunication.

You will always fully understand what one is trying to communicate and what one is going through. And you will always be able to be compassionate towards their experience and have empathy towards it because of that. We must return to a telepathic society, as it was intended and as we were all born.

All of the information that I have presented serves as an introduction and is meant to inspire you to do further research. I do not want you all to simply and blindly believe in everything that you read in this book. Do not just believe everything I tell you because it is me saying it or because it sounds nice, fancy, or intelligent.

What I want you to do is take this information and, instead of just believing in it blindly, do your own research and learn more about it. Make this information your own, to the point where you can express this information to anyone who asks you questions.

Gain this intelligence to have the capacity to fully integrate this knowledge and information.

Study and practice all I have mentioned up to this point.

Everything that I have included in this book is only part of the journey of information that I have gained and understood while living a spiritual journey in the past sixteen years of my life. I have learned so much more information than I have been able to fit into this book.

However, the information in this book, in particular, is what I felt was the most important thing that a human being needs to integrate and will come across anyway when they choose to walk the path of Brahmacharya.

When you make that conscious choice, intention, and decision to say, "I want to walk the path of becoming the ultimate human," the entire universe conspires from that point forward to bring you those experiences. All of creation will offer you the choices, the people, and the circumstances to bring you to that level.

You will start to get the training you need to get your mind to the point where it can become God-conscious and work from that place. So, you will start to attract tools of information with books like this one and many other books, videos, and documentaries, as well as interviews and people.

You will have all of these experiences, which you must now integrate into your consciousness to reach the ultimate form you are looking for, so that you can really end human suffering and move on to the next level of your soul's evolution.

Ultimately, you need to save yourself. Stop waiting for a savior to come and help you. No one is coming to save you.

You need to gain all the information, integrate it, and start applying it to your physical life yourself. This is how you save yourself, humanity! This is how it is done.

You cannot sit here and expect someone to come down from heaven and save you. It is not going to happen. Humans have been waiting for thousands of years, and they will continue to wait for billions of years if you let them.

You must influence humanity to realize that the power is within you. It is within us, all of us. We must awaken together. We must save ourselves. We must put ourselves to work. We must apply the knowledge. We must gain wisdom. We must create.

This is how humanity will save itself from those in power, whose very purpose is to awaken us in the first place.

The purpose of the elite and those who enslave humanity is to awaken humanity.

How ironic is that? They represent the shadow side, the shadow energy, of humanity's collective energy. As much as you may want to hate them, you must be grateful for their presence here on earth, for they are the reason humanity is finally awakening.

Everything that they have done to us and continue to do to us to this very day that you read this sentence, is designed to awaken us and help us continue to see through the illusions of separation and limitation. Every restriction they keep putting on us is meant to wake us up even more, to make us realize that we do not want a world with so many rules and restrictions, to make us realize that we do not want a small group of people to rule the rest of us, and to show us that we are smart and capable enough to rule ourselves.

Now that we know what we are capable of, we should experience less and less fear in our minds.

Once you have a complete astral projection experience, you will find yourself in the astral template of reality, where you can experience the spirit world firsthand. You will be able to understand what it is like to instantaneously manifest your experience, what it is like to float and levitate, what it is like to see colors you have no names for or to go through walls and matter, and what it is like to not have the four elements affect you in any way.

You will know what it is like to be free.

Once you experience this, you will lose your fear of dying. And once you lose the fear of death, you become a very powerful individual, because now, nothing can stop you. No one and nothing can stop you but you. You now have the full faith of a godlike being, which is what you need to do the work of *Spirit* on this planet without fear, hesitation, or any doubt that you can do it.

Once you are exposed to the awareness that *Mahasamadhi* exists and is an actual thing, well, now you will strive to attain that, because why would you want to die any other way? Why would you want to die by causing pain to yourself and your body? Why would you want to die because you got sick or because something bad happened to you? Why would you want to be murdered? Why would you want to experience any of that? Why would you not want to leave this earth through Mahasamadhi once you are exposed to this practice and the fact that it is possible for any human being? Why would you not?

From this point forward, even if you do not achieve Mahasamadhi in this lifetime, your soul will always desire it, even if you need to come back three more times. At this point, that seed has been planted in your consciousness, in your soul's journey on earth. From this point on, your soul will always want to reach Mahasamadhi until it gets there.

I pray, and it is my biggest prayer that all of you right now reading this will attain Mahasamadhi in this lifetime.

Once you have been exposed to the Maharishi effect and understand the power of meditation, you will forever meditate for the rest of your lifetime, and you will start influencing those in your family to do it. If you have children, you will begin to talk to your children about it and try to implement it in their daily lives. If you do not have kids yet, when you start to have children, you are going to raise them with this desire to meditate as it is born within them.

That is it, guys! Reading this book will forever change your life. It will forever affect the way that you view humanity. It will forever affect the way that you view yourself. It will affect the way that you raise your family from this point forward.

There is no going back to the old days of ignorance. You know better now.

You now know the full potential of a human being. You know, through meditation, through *Spirit*, through science, and by applying what we gained through the spiritual journey. You know what it is now. There is no excuse for not becoming the ultimate human.

We should all strive to become the ultimate human, to be our best selves. Once you understand what shadow work is and that you need to engage in it in order to heal and become a better version of yourself, you are going to start taking it more seriously. You might say, "All right, let me heal my trauma. Let me heal my pain. It is time for me to step in and fully embody the true potential of this human form. Why else did I come here? I did not come here to get a nine-to-five job, to become rich, or to travel the world, and that is it! I did not come here for those things."

There is a deeper meaning to the human experience. There is a reason why we need money to be comfortable. Money gives us the comfort, safety, and security we need to go out and learn about everything the world has to offer, as well as the means to pursue our interests and hobbies.

Money is not just so that we can buy expensive things and flaunt them, to praise the ego and make the ego feel better, or to make oneself look better or bigger than everyone else. We have all been programmed to do the wrong things with our abundance. And it is time to end those silly things. It is time to start taking life more seriously by having more fun.

Does that make sense? Please take life more seriously by having more fun, literally.

As you begin to have more fun, you start taking your life more seriously. How funny is that?

Once you have gone through your spiritual awakening, there is no going back. You will never be the same person again. But that is not a bad thing, so do not be sad. It is actually a good thing. You are becoming more of who you are, and you are shedding the illusion of who you thought you were.

You have been lying to yourself your whole life, but it is not your fault. You were programmed this way. You grew up in a world that forced you to be this way. But enough is enough. It is now time to shed those layers of illusion about who you are. It is now time for you to reconnect and tune back into the divine. It is time for you to act from a place of unconditional love as the most intelligent part of creation. It is time for you to see your potential, to see your worth, to increase your confidence, to increase your attitude, your mood, and your overall personality, to be a Brahmacharya, one who seeks the ultimate path.

We are the *Spirit* Ninjas. We work for *Spirit*, and we are infinite beings who have done this on many planets. We will continue to do so until we no longer wish to. That is the joy of *Spirit*. *Spirit* has free will. *Spirit* can exist in multi-dimensional realities simultaneously. We are omnipresent beings. We only choose to stay in these little physical bodies for a short time so that we can experience being physical and gain more soul experience.

Once you have learned about Paramahansa Yogananda's life, you will also know more about what the human experience can be.

For a man to experience what Paramahansa Yogananda did in the early 1900s, such things do not just go away. The experiences that human beings were capable of having back then do not simply go away. If anything, we can do more now than what they were capable of doing back then, because the energies on the earth today are greater in terms of spiritual essence and in terms of cosmic frequencies being bombarded on the earth today.

These powers are greater now. People can do much more than what the spiritual masters of that time were able to do. We can achieve much more in our time. We are accelerating our consciousness with every day that passes and with every generation that is born.

We are accelerating as humanity continues to evolve. Every new generation is smarter than the last one. It will stay this way until all of humanity rises to the highest level it can reach as a whole.

Once you have been exposed to the Kardashev scale, it will open your mind to the potential of what civilizations can become. It will hopefully inspire you all collectively to say, "Let's attain this or let's achieve that. Let's do it."

Nothing is stopping us from achieving these higher levels of being. We need to just work together; we need to lose the attitude of competition and competitiveness. There is nothing wrong with healthy competition and having fun doing it. It becomes a problem once you take it personally and seriously enough to the point that an illusion of separation is created.

Competition becomes unhealthy when you create anger, anguish, or envy between you and the individuals who are interacting with you. This is when it becomes a problem. When you try it out, you wear each other down. This is when it becomes a problem, because now it is causing separation. It is causing darkness to arise within you to create that separation.

Healthy competition is beautiful. There is nothing wrong with being competitive and having fun. There is nothing wrong with that. But we need to lose the energy of competitiveness that drives us to diminish one another. These are the things we need to lose collectively.

Practicing greater empathy and compassion in order to have it in us—to understand what the other person is going through and what they are trying to express—will lead to us collectively becoming more compassionate people.

We need to be compassionate, guys. There is no reason to be envious or hateful. You need to have compassion in your heart, so that way, you can understand everyone's experience on earth. It will help you learn to love people more and to trust them again.

I believe a lot of people are only after money. Everyone, especially in America, is just trying to get by, survive, or level up. You absolutely fall into one of these categories. Either you are just trying to get by and survive, or you are trying to level up and increase more of what you already have.

But what happens when you start to have it all? What happens when you do achieve the financial and material success that your ego and mind yearn to experience? What comes after that? What comes next? It depends on the frequency level of the people who have attained this type of success.

If they vibrate at a low frequency in terms of still failing within the illusion of separation, still trying to be competitive and show off what they have, then that individual will get to the point where they will be capable of exploiting humanity.

When someone has that much money and power but does not have the frequency of love or the desire to share what they know to help everyone else, they will go down a path where they use their money and power to take advantage of people.

But if you are a person who wants to share, uplift, and

support humanity so that they can also reach the level of success that this person has reached, then your money and success will lead you down the path of trying to understand the nature of reality and spirituality; how reality works.

This will lead you to understand what densities and dimensions are and how they operate, which is a chapter I chose to dedicate to all of you.

So now you have a better understanding of the nature of reality and how it all operates. Physical reality is constructed of energy, vibration, and frequency. This has already been proven scientifically, and many people understand this now.

But when you apply that information to how you view every second of your life, well, then you start to perceive your reality differently; you start to see it for what it is. You begin to recognize it for what it is: energy vibrating at a frequency.

When you start to perceive reality in this way, you start to protect your energy more. You start to look into things that can protect your energy, like crystals, sage, Palo Santo, chanting mantras, or learning deeper meditation. You do whatever you have to do to protect your energy.

You must be aware that you live in a dualistic world where it is very easy to get sucked into other people's universes. It is very easy to get sucked into the downward spiral emotionally, mentally, and spiritually in which you sabotage yourself, your progress, and your *Spirit*.

It is very easy to get sucked into the negativity that surrounds you. In duality, it can be hard to learn how to stay centered in your light, but this is a challenge that will help you grow and move on to the next stage of your soul's evolution.

So, what more can I say to you all? I have given you everything that I felt was necessary to give you when you made that conscious decision to attract truth into your life; everything you needed to know was right here.

I have given you the tools you need to become the best kind of person on this planet, like a real-life superhero, avatar, or yogi who can say and do things that most people cannot. You have the skills to be someone who is humble enough to teach others what they have learned to attain this same level of mastery.

We will all gain a sense of responsibility once we gain superpowers. That responsibility will be to learn how to control our superpowers, how to be humble, how to help those in need, and how to teach and educate those who are willing to receive the information. This is the responsibility of every conscious human being.

Please look at me as an individual who is capable of guiding others back to *Spirit*, back to the Divine. I am nothing more than that. Please do not ever look at me as a being who is above anyone else on this planet. I am no more special than any human being reading and listening to these words right now. I am no better than any of you.

We are all equal at the level of our souls. We are helping each other back home. All I want to be for humanity is a guide back towards the infinite, a guide to help you realize and understand your true potential, a guide who can help bring you back to god-consciousness.

This book is a guidebook of information that a person might come across in the future as they embark on the path of becoming the ultimate human. This is the information you will learn to know, understand, and integrate. This is also the information you will, one day, begin to share with people, or perhaps a huge group of people. This is what humanity is missing.

Humanity is missing the pieces of information included in this book. When enough of us know and understand this information, we will, without a doubt, choose to embark on this path.

Everyone wants to end their suffering. Everyone wants to be happy. Everyone wants to feel fulfilled. So, it is a non-sequitur to start down this path if you know it exists but do not care where it goes. But it does make sense to start this journey in the full knowledge that your light will become a torch for others to follow.

Once you know there is more for you to experience, you can live a happier, healthier, more fulfilled life. Why would you not want that? It would be insane not to want that.

Hey guys, that is actually okay. If you do not want that, then that is your path in this lifetime. There is nothing wrong with that. Remember that you will have a lifetime—an incarnation—when this will become more and more intriguing to you.

Ultimately, you are going to get what you need from this book—nothing more, nothing less. Whatever you do not want to accept after reading this book, or whatever does not resonate with you from this book, it is totally okay. You will get what you need somewhere else.

However, if you have read this far, you were meant to read this book, point blank, period. It is meant to be a part of your subconscious and conscious minds. You now have this fully integrated and downloaded into your mind.

You are in Chapter Eleven, guys. You are here. We did this together.

This was a journey for me to write, and this was a

journey for you to read. Trust me, I know. We are reflections of each other. I am in your position right now. I have been in your position countless times.

But I now find myself in a new position as an author. I am the one who is actually writing the information that a collective group of people is reading.

I think this is amazing.

This is beautiful.

I have never done something like this.

I have written hundreds of songs and performed them in front of hundreds and thousands of people throughout my life, but I have never written anything that a large number of people will read. It is something they will be able to read in twenty, thirty, fifty, or perhaps one hundred thousand years. This is pretty dope. I really love this.

And I do not know if I will write another book or not, but I do know one thing: at least I wrote one, and that is enough for me.

I am grateful to have had this experience.

I am grateful to be in a position to do so.

I am thankful to be in a position to have my words touch millions of human beings. It is a blessing, and I am eternally grateful to *Spirit*, the universe, God, and humanity.

I hope you finish this book feeling a little kinder, a little more confident, a little happier, a little more in tune with the frequency of love, and a little more hopeful for humanity's future. It is all about you. Everything in this world is about you.

It is all for you, from you, and to you. Even though this book was written by you for you, I love you. I believe in you. I want you to become better. This is your favorite infinite being, CrewZ, signing out. I will see you on the other side. The End.

Musical Vibes for this chapter

Search: **CrewZ - The Ancients**

https://song.link/us/i/1465340415

Acknowledgments

I would like to thank my mentor and friend, Billy Carson, for suggesting the idea of a book, which grew into a whole new process of mind-expanding communication for me.

Thank you to all my fans who connect with me, driving me to greater heights in my music and now my writing.
    There's so much more to come.

About the Author

Kenny Garcia, well known as CrewZ, is an emerging author sharing what it takes to become the Ultimate Human.

In his words, "My whole reason for becoming an author is to uplift and inspire people. I want everyone to not only reach their fullest potential as human beings, but I also want each of you to learn how to embody that amazing positive pathway during your earthly experience."

CrewZ's goal of expansion can also be heard mixed into his music where he enjoys rapping and singing about concepts that expand and empower the human mind. "Through my music, you are empowering yourself with affirmations. All you need to do to gain this superhuman support is repeat my words."

A few quick details about CrewZ are:

- Born and raised in Long Island New York
- Moved to Florida mid junior year of high school
- of Colombian descent
- spiritual awakening journey began at eighteen

Full of endless creativity, CrewZ enjoys drawing, playing instruments, maintaining a fitness lifestyle, and being a father. "I'm very into studying and learning about ancient civilizations as well as understanding quantum or cosmic topics." Most of his days are spent enjoying Nature.

"As for the future," says CrewZ, "I look forward to sharing with you my art, my music, and any expressive form in my creations that inspires and empowers us all as humans."

Social Media

JOIN AND FOLLOW CREWZ

Hello, all you free thinkers. I believe you are like me. I know you want to take back control of your life and your destiny. And from that place of abundance, you will learn the mysteries behind what humans must do in order to expand their consciousness.

Anyone who is into upgrading their lives to the next level of human existence can follow me.

Spotify: https://open.spotify.com/
artist/
4yIBmnW8bMq1V0C2N0Z1pb?
si=
pQKt3o8PRFS1aVEB79TRHg&
utm_source=copy-link

Instagram: https://instagram.com/
crewzthroughlife?igshid=
YmMyMTA2M2Y=

YouTube channel: https://www.youtube.com/@
crewzthroughlife

Meditation course: https://meditatewithcrewz.thinkific.com/

As mentioned in *The Ultimate Human, Chapter 7,* for any readers who are interested in learning how to breathe properly through their diaphragm, along with the other beautiful spiritual practices that help guide them into further enlightenment, please visit the link above. When you visit this link, you will be able to view and purchase this course.

Printed in Great Britain
by Amazon

35257019R00089